Gilbert Ashville Pierce

Zachariah, the Congressman

a tale of American society

Gilbert Ashville Pierce

Zachariah, the Congressman
a tale of American society

ISBN/EAN: 9783337023669

Printed in Europe, USA, Canada, Australia, Japan

Cover: Foto ©Suzi / pixelio.de

More available books at **www.hansebooks.com**

MR. EBENEZER BARNCASTLE.

ZACHARIAH,

THE CONGRESSMAN;

A Tale of American Society.

BY

GILBERT A. PIERCE.

CHICAGO:

DONNELLEY, GASSETTE & LOYD, PUBLISHERS.

1880.

CONTENTS.

ZACHARIAH, THE CONGRESSMAN.

CHAPTER I.

IN WHICH ZACHARIAH MAKES HIS FIRST APPEAR-
ANCE.

" But suppose there are two mobs," suggested Mr. Snodgrass.
" Shout with the largest," replied Mr. Pickwick.

" Three cheers for Zachariah Martin ! "

" Hurrah, hurrah, hurrah ! "

" Tiger ! "

" Rah-h-h ! "

Behold the hubbub in Hiltonville ! The people are awake. The boys are excited.

The country band has assembled in front of
the town hall, and Slim Timothy Bobbin is whirling around and making himself observed from all
observable points. Slim Timothy Bobbin is in
some respects responsible for this confusion. In

1*

9

this wise: The Congressional convention is just ended. Two prominent candidates have been before the convention, and the strife between them has waxed high. Numerous papers had declared for Israel Snapp, and held aloft the name of Snapp to an admiring world. Numerous other papers had hoisted the name of Simpson and proclaimed his virtues to the public.

"Where will you find another man who unites to a masterly intellect a heart as tender as a woman's and a love for the common people which can not be questioned or denied." Thus the "Herald of Liberty" for Snapp.

The "Register of Freedom," on the other hand, held a different opinion. "Mr. Simpson," said that organ, "is peculiarly fitted for this high position. His commanding ability as a stump-speaker is recognized throughout the State. During the war his trumpet-tongued eloquence was heard on every side like the mighty rushing of many waters, and he was only restrained from mingling in the conflict himself by the unfortunate illness of his son Ichabod. Now, however, Mr. Simpson is all for peace, and his efforts, if elected, will be directed toward restoring fraternal feeling to the distracted land."

But, alas! for Snapp, and alas! for Simpson. Twenty ballots were had, and each time there was a tie. Neither faction would give way. In this crisis, a patriotic citizen who had mildly supported Snapp arose. "He deprecated strife in this great and glorious party. He would sacrifice personal preference to unity and harmony. [Applause by the Simpson men, who thought he was coming over to them.] Every man here was a patriot. [Immense applause by all.] They had proven it by standing to their colors throughout a score of campaigns. And should they desert them now? [Cries of "No, no!"] Where there had been unity should there be division? Sooner let his name perish from the earth." He closed by withdrawing the name of Snapp, and nominating as a substitute one upon whom all could unite; one who, though young in years, was known and loved, and one whose brilliant entrance on the political stage cast a shadow on many an older politician. He nominated, as a candidate for this position, Zachariah Martin, Esq., of Pine County.

And Timothy Bobbin had thrown his hat high up in the air at this, and screamed himself hoarse in his enthusiasm.

Who would have believed it? Observe the fickleness of the human heart! Fifty men had sworn eternal allegiance to Snapp. They forsook him for Zachariah. As many more had vowed never to forsake Simpson. They went over to the new man in a body, and, in precisely twenty minutes from the time his name was announced, Zachariah Martin was the candidate of the convention for Congress.

Zachariah Martin was a young man, not yet twenty-seven, and the son of a well-to-do farmer who had gotten his property by hard work, and knew what it had cost him. He was very proud of Zach., and had given him a very good education at the "High School" in the neighboring town,

but his highest ambition went no farther than to
have his son one of the first men in the county
the richest farmer in it, and, perhaps, President of
the Agricultural Society. For politics he cared,
very little, and, although he now and then got
excited in times of great popular outbreaks, and
generally voted the straight ticket, yet he was
accustomed to say "that the whole thing was a
confounded humbug," and he had no time to talk
about it. Not so, however, with his wife, Zach.'s
mother. Though a hard-working woman, and one
tolerably ignorant of anything relating to affairs
of state, she always had a notion that Zach. would
become a great man of some kind, and industriously courted favor with every one having the
least pretension to prominence.

"I allers stuck to it," said she, "that *my* children should go among the foremost, or not go at
all;" and so it happened that when Zach. began to
display a taste for politics, and when he rose
through successive campaigns to be, first, chairman
of the Township Campaign Club; then, member of

the County Central Committee; then, a delegate to the State Convention, the old lady's pride rose with him, until it grew unrestrainable as Zach. stood upon the platform at a great mass meeting and introduced to the assembled multitude the party's candidate for Governor. When that candidate turned around on the platform and referred in complimentary terms to his "esteemed friend Mr. Martin," the good lady could scarcely refrain from shouting outright. She nodded her head at every sentence, and looked from the speaker to Zach., and back again and smiled and "hunched" Mrs. Whitcomb, who sat next her, until her husband gruffly told her not to make a fool of herself, his usual way of addressing her whenever anything in her manner displeased him.

But Zach. grew in political knowledge, and two years before this story opens had made a canvass of the State and been quite successful as a speaker. He was being seriously talked of for Congress by a few ardent admirers in his own county, but there had been no effort made to bring his name before the convention, save by a few, until, as narrated above, a lucky incident threw him into the breach as a compromise candidate, and he was nominated.

Zach. had no serious thought of being selected, still he knew that it was just possible he might be, and he was in a feverish excitement during the day that the convention was held. "Of course I don't expect they'll do it," he said to his mother, standing in his shirt sleeves, leaning up against the kitchen door, while she industriously scoured the knives and forks. "I don't expect they'll do it, but it will be funny if something *does* occur to make me the choice."

"They're plaguey fools if they don't, that's all I have to say," replied his mother, carefully wiping the table and setting things to rights. "Plaguey fools if they don't."

"Who's plaguey fools?" said the old gentleman, coming in the outer door.

"Them convention men if they don't nominate Zach.," said the old lady, lighting her pipe.

"Tut, tut, old woman, here's more foolishness," replied Mr. Martin. "I allers hoped Zach. would settle down on the farm and stay with us, but it seems his head is bent on destruction. I don't like these politicians anyhow. I mind how smooth and oily Snyder was when he was running for Sheriff. Called on us frequent. Even went out one night and helped milk the cows, and said nothing would suit him better than to take a hand at husking. But, dang it! he didn't know me t'other day when he met me in town; and that's the way with 'em all. I wouldn't have a thing to do with 'em, Zach., if I was you; not a thing."

Zach. only smiled as his father ceased speaking, and walked away; but the old lady shook her head, and remarked that "Joe never did care about anything better than raising corn and calves. As for her, she wanted her children eddicated, and she wanted them to be something, and a precious lot they'd a' been, she guessed, if they'd a follered his advice, and if she hadn't seen to 'em."

The day wore away, and it was night, and as

no news had been received Zach concluded that
the expected candidate had been nominated. The
little town of Martin's Corners, near which they
lived, was very quiet, and nine o'clock had arrived,
when all at once shouts were heard in the village,
and soon afterward the sound of a fife and drum
followed, intermingled with more shouts. A few
minutes afterward a buggy, furiously driven, came
up the road, and in a minute more stopped before
the farm-house. Two men were in it, and as they
leaped to the ground they shouted:

"Hurrah for Martin!"

Zach.'s heart beat as he looked from the window. One of the men hastily tied the horse, and
as he finished the other one took off his hat and
cried out, "Three cheers for Martin," which were
given by the twain with a will, and which were
echoed from the village with still louder cheers.
The men came to the door, which was opened by
Mr. Martin, and as they walked in Zach. recognized
one of them as the Hon. Aaron Spiker, who had
been a livery stable keeper, a real estate agent, a

B

member of the Legislature, and a very chronic
office holder at Hiltonville, the county seat, but
who now lived at Martin's Corners. The other
was a quiet, mild-eyed little fellow, to whom we
have before alluded, by name Timothy Bobbin, a
gentleman engaged in no particular business that
any one ever heard of, but who was universally
respected for his non-combativeness. Spiker was
a stout man, with short hair and a very red face,
shaved smooth. He had an imposing shirt front
and wore gold studs, which lowered him several
degrees in old Mr. Martin's estimation. He
advanced and wrung Zach.'s hand with the ardor
of a long-separated brother.

"Zach.," said he, slapping him on the back and
wheezing with his great exertions, "You've got it,
old fellow! You're nominated!"

At this Zach. grasped the hand of Spiker with
great fervor, putting his left in both the hands of
Bobbin, who smiled, and stroked the honored
palm with much tenderness.

"We've done it, eh, Bobbin?" said Spiker.

"We've done it in spite of 'em all. You were nominated on the twenty-first ballot!"

"On the twenty-first ballot," echoed Bobbin.

"The fight was terrible, terrible," repeated Spiker, shaking his head and contracting his eyebrows, at which Bobbin shook his head and contracted *his* eye-brows, breaking off in the very middle of a smile to look serious.

"It was a terrible fight, but a few determined men put the thing through and won the day, eh Bobbin?"

Bobbin came out of his thunder - cloud of solemnity and rushed into the sunshine of merry recollection, and then Spiker shook hands with Mr. and Mrs. Martin, who, up to this time, had been wholly unnoticed, and was immediately followed in this ceremony by Bobbin.

"Yes, it was a hard fight," continued Spiker, turning again to Zach. "Oh, all kinds of objections were urged against you. 'He has no settled convictions,' says one. 'Hang the convictions,' says I. 'What do you want with him? Here's a

man goes to Congress to represent the people.
We can't all go, so we send a man. We're the
ones to have the principles, and he is the one to
enforce them. What the blue blazes has he got
to do with convictions;' eh, Bobbin? Ain't that
what I said?"

"Them's um," returned Bobbin.

"Another fellow says he, 'Martin may be a good
man, but he's too young; he lacks experience.'"

"'How do you count years in politics?' says I.
'If you count the Summers which he has seen
he is young, but if you count the wounds he has
given and the scars he has received in the service
of the party he is older than the best of us.'
That cracked his nut, didn't it, Bobbin?"

"Mashed him," replied Bobbin.

"Coming along, I says to Bobbin here," continued Spiker, "says I, 'I never worked harder for
a man than for Martin, and I'm very much mistaken if he forgets it. We've never had any patronage in this county. One of the best offices in
the district ought to come here,' and, says I, 'I'm

fooled if Zach. Martin ain't just the man to send
it here.' 'And if ever a man deserved that same
office,' says Bobbin to me, 'Aaron Spiker is that
man.' 'I've done nothing but my duty to my
country, Bobbin,' says I; but he insisted that my
part in the matter should be mentioned, and
threatened to do it himself, and he always blun-
ders so I thought it best to get ahead of him.
Eh, Bobbin? Ain't that so?"

"That's so," said Bobbin.

"I shall most assuredly remember you," said
Zach, warmly shaking the fat man's hand again.

"Thank you!" returned Spiker, "I can considered that settled then."

Zach. said "yes" without hesitation.

"The collector's office," said Spiker.

"You can have what you want," returned Zach
impulsively, and they again shook hands all
round.

"They are coming!" said the fat man, as the
sound of the drum drew nearer. "We stopped and
told them and they are coming, and we must have

a little speech from you." And as the old lady in
a terrible state of excitement threw open the front
door that led into the little parlor and lighted
both big lamps, the procession of nearly fifty men,
women, and children drew up at the door. The
fat man stepped out on the balcony as it stopped,
and cried out:

"Three cheers for your distinguished fellow-
citizen, Zachariah Martin," and the cheers were
given with great spirit.

"Fellow citizens," said Spiker, addressing the
crowd, "it is useless to inquire what air the circumstances that draw this spontaneous crowd from
their peaceful pursoots. What means this ere
procession and lights? What means this beat
of the drum and sound of the soul-stirring fife?
Is the Fourth of July upon us? No, my friends,
it does not mean that. The great American
nation looks with pride upon Martin's Corners
to-night, for it has furnished a statesman, a young
man it is true, but one whose name will yet stand
bright on the roll of — that is to say — patriots.

Need I say who it is? I see the answer beforehand in your eyes. I read it in your looks. It is
your own townsman, Zachariah Martin, who I now
have the pleasure of introducing to you."

At this Spiker stepped back, while the crowd
cheered lustily as Zach. advanced. He made a
speech neither good nor bad, but one which bore
evident marks of having been thought about
beforehand, under a possibility that he might be
the lucky man. He of course said it was the
proudest moment of his life, which was true, and
that he had never dreamed of such an honor,
which was not true. He declared that *he* was
nothing; that the nomination was not a tribute
to him personally, but to the great principles he
advocated, and closed by promising the crowd that
his life should be devoted to their service and in
upholding the liberties of his countrymen. Then
there were hand-shakings, and more congratulations, and a repetition by Spiker of the scenes at
the convention, and at last the crowd separated,
and Zach. was alone with his father and mother.

"Well!" exclaimed he, taking a hand of each, "what do you think now? Ain't I getting up in the world pretty fast?"

"Not a bit," said his mother, settling herself back rather stiffly; "I know'd it. I said so ever since you was born. Even while you was kicking and crowing in my lap, says I, 'Joe,' says I, 'that boy has a head on him that's a plaguey sight mor'n common,' and so it was."

Zach. smiled good-naturedly, and pressed his mother's hand.

"Well, Zach.," spoke up his father, "it's a big thing, I. s'pose. Anyway, I'm proud of you. But I've seen these great men in my time. They went away with big hopes. Some of 'em got mighty proud and stuck up, but arter a while they growed fretful, and two of 'em died in rags, arter all they had flown so high. I'm not going to discourage you, Zach., but I stick to it that a living got by honest work is the manly and independent way arter all."

"Oh, you'll feel different when you see my

name heralded through the land, and my praise in every mouth," said Zach.

"Yes, I s'pose so," replied his father; "but no matter how bright the outside of this public life may look, it is full of disappointments and vexation, and it may come to you, my boy; it may come to you."

"That's the way!" broke in Mrs. Martin rather testily, "allers a-humbugging and a-prophesying."

"Never mind," said Zach., laughing, "we won't cross the river till we get to it, anyway."

And the trio fell into plans for the future, and discussed them till long after the usual hour for retiring. So the first evening of Zach.'s greatness passed, and it was well on toward the dawn of the next day before his overtaxed nerves became sufficiently composed to permit him to sleep.

2

CHAPTER II.

IN WHICH PEGGY CLOVER MAKES HER BOW.

"Where can Peggy be?" said Zach. to his mother, coming into the house next morning from a long communion outside with himself. "It's certainly time she was home."

"Nobody knows," replied his mother. "Trapesing over the hills like a wild Indian, I suppose. Nothing would do but she must go over to the Fairweathers yesterday morning, to stay all night with the girls. She promised to be home before breakfast this morning, and here it is ten o'clock and not a sign of her yet. The girl is getting too trifling for anything."

"I believe I will go out and find her," said Zach., partly to himself, and partly to his mother. "I know her haunts, and I'll bring her in."

Mrs. Martin took her hands out of a washbowl and, looking straight at Zach., said: " I wouldn't do it, Zach. Folks have allers thought it strange how you run after her, and it'll be a mighty sight stranger now. You ought to look higher. She's nothing, and she never will be."

Old Mr. Martin had approached while the conversation was going on, and broke in now.

"She's an honest girl," said he; "good enough for a king, that's what she is; and I say that a man who will give up an honest girl just because he is like to get a little office ought to be shot as a deserter, and I hope that'll be the first law you pass when you get to Congress."

"Now you're both right," said Zach. "Peggy has not been thought a good match for me, and no one would blame me now for looking in another direction; but you both know I love Peggy, and I do not intend to give her the go-by, because I've been lucky. But of course she must improve herself. It will be no little thing to be the wife of a member of the United States Congress, and she'll see that as well as anybody. If

she has a mind to, no one will have reason to be
ashamed of Peggy Clover. I'm going to meet
her. She hasn't heard a word yet, I'll be bound,
and I'll startle her out of her wits," and away Zach.
went down a path that led toward the grove.

"The idea of Zach.'s marrying that girl," said
Mrs. Martin, "when there haint a born lady in the
land but would jump at the chance of him."

"Betsy!" said the old man, "you're a fool.
What's a born lady with no soul, and no body to
speak of, compared to a healthy, blooming lass,
with a heart bigger than an ox, and steel springs
in every limb. Suppose she can't simper and
giggle, and wear bustles bigger than a haystack.
She can work, and she can love, and what's better,
she can be true and faithful to the end, and that's
what some of your born ladies can't do, let me tell
you. Lord! what a girl that is for business. If
Zach. had only stayed on the farm and married
Peggy I'd a made over my whole property to
them. But he never will be contented till he's
gone through the mill."

Zach. wandered away down the path, and as he neared the grove peered through under the trees, expecting to get a sight of Miss Peggy returning.

Peggy Clover was an orphan, and had as good as been brought up by the Martin family. She first turned up as a waif at the little tavern in the village, where, at the age of nine, she was washing dishes, building fires, and otherwise paying her way. She came into the country with her father, a sort of itinerant portrait painter, who sought the locality for his health, and endeavored to meet the wants of himself and child by occasional jobs in his line. But there were few who cared for anything as grand as a painted picture among the simple, practical folk of that region, and so Mr. Clover's customers were few, and his earnings very pitiful. He boarded at the little public house, and when the unfortunate man yielded to his disease and went peacefully to his long sleep, in debt to the proprietor, Peggy was the sole dependence of that worthy gentleman out of which to get his money back. He kept her ostensibly because the poor little thing had no other home, but really because she was wonderfully handy about the house, and did an astonishing amount of work in an incredibly short space of time; and gradually more and more came to be piled on the willing little worker until, overtasked, she fell very ill and her life was despaired of. The doctor's bills began to look formidable, and there being funeral expenses in prospect, the hotel keeper was only too glad to accept the proposition of the Martins to take her home, nurse her, and if she recovered, adopt her. She soon got up and was regarded as a very lucky girl to be taken into the wealthiest and most influential family in the neighborhood. She had to work, to be sure, for all in that region worked, no matter what their circumstances; but she was used to that, and as she grew to understand that the Martins' home was hers, the first she had ever had, she was happy at the thought and happy in the enjoyment of it. She went to school during the short season it was in session and had certainly grown up a promising young lady.

From the very first Zach. had been her friend, and the twain, from the affection of a brother and sister, had gradually come to experience a stronger feeling, a love rarely expressed, scarcely understood, even by themselves, and yet some way settled and stored away in their hearts as a matter fully arranged and consummated. Zach. fully expected to marry her, she fully expected to be Zach.'s wife, yet exactly when had never entered either of their heads. Zach. had carried himself a little high when he returned to the farm from an academical course which he had taken in a neighboring town, but he soon lowered when Peggy, with a woman's tact, pretended to be interested in another young gentleman of the village; and so the old relations were renewed. And thus they had gone on, Zach. entering into politics ardently and securing considerable reputation thereby, Peggy looking upon it all as a matter of course, proud of him, to be sure, but no more so than if he never had been heard of outside of their own little neighborhood. There was a vein of frivolity, or rather rompishness, about Peggy that Zach., as he became more impressed with his own dignity and possibilities, disliked. She could row on the lake as well as the champion oarsman of the village. She could leap a fence quicker than half of the boys, and in a race was most astonishingly fleet of foot. She could sing, but she sang songs that grated upon Zach.'s ear, especially after his return from school, and all these things he strove to correct in her. She would listen demurely, and promise sacredly, but she forgot the compact before the words were cold, and was skimming across the fields ere the echo of Zach.'s tones had scarcely died away, Zach. felt on the morning in question that a more solemn interview than ever was necessary, and had determined to make an impression on her that would be lasting. He had reached a little opening in the path and seated himself on a log to await her coming, and there he sat when he was awakened from a reverie

by her voice. She was concealed by the thick
foliage that shaded the pathway, but her tones
were distinctly audible. She was singing as she
walked, and Zach. detected an absurd break or
twitch in the lines every now and then which he
shrewdly guessed was occasioned by a nervous
hop, skip, and jump, which Peggy was fond of
indulging in as an accompaniment to her music.
She was "humming" the song, the words of which,
if words they could be called, sounded something
like this:

> Then blow ye winds hi-o,
>   Tra la la la lay;
> I'm going to my own true love
>   A thousand miles away a-a.

"Now such a song as that," said Zach. to himself, "How that would sound at the Russian
Minister's or the Secretary of State's! Can't the
girl learn anything?"

As Zach. thought this aloud, Peggy appeared
bounding along the path. She stopped short with
a little screech upon seeing Zach., then, drawing

back, puckered her mouth, and gave vent to a low whistle.

"Well," said she, finally, "if there ain't Zach."

"Yes, here's Zach.," responded that worthy.

"Why, what you doing here?" said Peggy.

"Come after you," replied Zach.

"Oh, what a nice little boy he is getting to be," said Peggy, and she patted him on the cheek good-humoredly.

Zach. took her hand in his, and looking very serious, said: "Peggy, I want to talk to you — to talk soberly, too. Now, you know whistling will do for a cow-boy, but you're not a cow-boy, are you?"

"I believe not," said Peggy.

"Then, not being a cow-boy, you ought not to act like one," he went on.

"Well, that's settled," returned Peggy. "No more whistling for me. Now, what else?"

"I suppose you haven't heard the news," said Zach., assuming an air of indifference.

"No. What is it?" she inquired with woman's eagerness.

"You haven't heard it?" said Zach., almost reproachfully, "while everybody else knows. Well, guess."

"You've found my rabbits," said Peggy, quickly.

Zach. looked at her almost contemptuously. "Your rabbits!" he said. "Well, no, it isn't that; guess again."

Peggy rolled her eyes, with a thoughtful expression, upward, and then said, half inquiringly —

"Mrs. Miles is dead."

Zach. shook his head with rather of a disappointed air. It was plain she hadn't a thought of what had really happened, though he had told her repeatedly that the prospect was open to him, and he so wished that she would take an interest in these things.

"No," said he. "Mrs. Miles is not dead. It is something about me."

"Something about you?" said she. "I know! you've had that tooth pulled," and she seized him by the chin with her right hand, while she went to inspecting his mouth with her left. Zach. took

away her hands laughing in spite of himself.
"There, there!" said he, "you'll never guess; let
me tell you. I have been nominated for Congress."

"You've been what?" exclaimed Peggy.

"Nominated for Congress," said Zach., "and, of
course, shall be elected. I am going to have a
great office, Peggy."

"Oh! I heard about that," said Peggy, rather
contemptuously.

"You heard of it," returned Zach., "and didn't
you wonder at it?"

"Why, is it such a dreadful thing?" said
she.

"Now, look here, Peggy," exclaimed Zach., "let's
have a serious talk about this. I shall soon be
elected to one of the highest-positions in the land. ·
I shall go to Washington and associate with great
people, fine ladies and eminent men, shall visit the
President and Judges of the Supreme Court, and
walk arm in arm with them."

"I wouldn't do it, Zach., said Peggy, solemnly.

"You wouldn't do it?" he cried. "How would

you like to go with me, and be dressed in silks and satins, like Cinderela?"

"Oh, crackey!" exclaimed Peggy, clapping her hands, "but you're joking, Zach."

"No, I'm not, and that's just what I want to talk to you about; and don't you see, Peggy, that your manners here would not do there? In those refined circles no slang or vulgarity are allowed, and you use both."

"Why, Zach.!" cried Peggy, amazed, "I *never!* What did I ever say that was vulgar?"

"I do not mean immoral," said Zach., "but low. You must leave off expressions which offend polite ears. I heard you say 'Oh, crackey' just now. Very well. 'Oh, crackey' will do for Martin's Corners, but it won't do for Washington.

"I'll never say it again, Zach.," said Peggy, looking penitent.

"Well, it's not that alone," Zach. went on. "All these rough words and songs must be left off. Now what was that I heard you singing just now?"

Peggy hung her head and looked a little sheepish.

"That was a funny little song we heard at the show," said she. "I heard you say you liked it."

"Yes, but such songs won't do for you," he answered. "I told you once before they wouldn't do. You sing, and sing well, but you must choose something more genteel, you know. Then there is another thing. You must quit calling me Zach."

At this Peggy looked at him in perfect amazement. "Quit calling you Zach.!" she burst out. "Why, what on earth shall I call you?"

"Call me Mr. Martin," said he.

"Mr. Mar——." Here Peggy fairly roared. "Mr. Martin! Oh, crackey!" And it was so funny that Peggy laughed the tears into her eyes.

"There you go again with your 'Oh, crackey!'" said Zach. pettishly.

"I didn't quite get it out, Zach.—Mr. Martin," responded Peggy, stammering, and correcting herself.

"Well, you act as if there was something

immensely funny about calling me by my name," said he. "How do you think it would sound to have you rush through the rooms at the President's reception, bawling 'Zach., oh, Zach.?'"

"'Twould sound dreadful, wouldn't it?" said Peggy, thoughtfully imagining the effect. "But then Zach. has always been so dear to me, and to call you Mr. Martin seems so cold. It seems to me they must be very heartless down there, no matter how grand they are; but I shall call you Mr. Martin after this, see if I don't."

"Well," said Zach., a little less confidently, "try to look at these things right, Peggy, that's all. You don't want to be laughed at, I know, and I want you to eclipse everybody when you go to the capital as my wife; that's all — it's for you I say these things."

"Zach.," said Peggy, very resolutely, "I'll learn to do everything you say."

"That's right," exclaimed Zach., pressing her hands warmly; "and when you go down there we shall be the happiest mortals alive. You shall have dresses with forty yards of silk in them, and be decked in diamonds like a princess. You shall have your carriage and your servants, and the people will say 'there goes the beautiful and accomplished Mrs. Zach. Martin.'"

"And you will be my husband?" said Peggy, her thoughts running away from the finery to the one great desire of her heart.

"I shall be your husband," said Zach., "and you shall be my wife, and here's a kiss to start it with," and Zach. drew her slender form to him and kissed her most tenderly.

"Ah! we shall be so happy," sighed Peggy, dreamily. 'So happy, and I owe it all to you, Zach., all to you." And she said the "Zach." so tenderly, and crept to him so confidingly, that he did not reprove her. The ship was sailing away freely now, no signs of storm, and they, with hearts that beat so high, were sailing with it.

CHAPTER III.

BOBBIN'S HOME AND HOPES.

When Spiker and Bobbin drove away from the Martins', on the night of the speech-making, it was in the best of spirits. Spiker was happy over Zach.'s promise, and Bobbin was happy in a sort of reflected way because of Spiker's happiness. When the two reached the village they alighted and started to their respective homes. Spiker opened a gate before a pretentious house, and with his overcoat across his arm stalked down the graveled walk with an air of authority. Bobbin sped around to a back street, and, with his pinched coat buttoned up, directed his steps toward a little one-story house that had an air of begging to exist, and in its jammed and battered appearance bore a striking resemblance to little Bobbin himself. He raised the latch and walked in, sniffing his nose approvingly as he caught the smell of supper. The meal was ready and Mrs. Bobbin was waiting for him. Four children, so near of a size that it seemed necessary to number them to distinguish one from the other, were clustered round her, tugging at her dress and demanding that the eating should begin. Mrs. Bobbin was a thin, unhealthy-looking woman, whose clothes seemed only put on for the sake of decency, and to be constantly threatening to fall off. She had a tired air, and looked as if she had had a weary dispute with the world and been floored. Bobbin himself was in high spirits this evening, and he gave the family a kiss all round with the air of a prince scattering gold among the poor.

"You're awful late," observed Mrs. Bobbin.

"Thought you'd never come," said the oldest child, as they seated themselves at the supper table.

"We had the *biggest* time," said the little man, rubbing his hands as he sat down, "about the biggest time, Elvira, you ever heard of. You ought to have seen me and Spiker work. It was always Spiker and Bobbin. Nothing could be done without Spiker and Bobbin. Finally we beat the crowd and nominated — who now do you think?"

"Oh, I heard," said Mrs. B.

"Zach. Martin," said Bobbin; "yes, Zach. It was about the biggest victory for me and Spiker we ever had."

"I should think you'd get tired of it," said Mrs. Bobbin.

"Tired nothing!" said Bobbin. "It's the biggest fun out, especially when you win. Really, this nomination is my doing, for I was the first one to suggest Zach., and it run like wild-fire."

"Well, I suppose he's satisfied now," said his wife.

"Not yet," returned Bobbin; "there's the campaign ahead yet, and it's going to be a lively one; but we'll elect Zach. if it takes the skin off."

"Do you think he'll thank you for it?" said Mrs. Bobbin.

"Thank us!" exclaimed Bobbin. "You don't

know Zach.   Now, I'll tell you something private, but don't let it go an inch further.   Spiker and I were the first to take the news to him, and when Spiker told him how we had worked, you never saw a man so grateful.   He took each of us by the hand, and promised Spiker the Collector's office sure."

"Promised Spiker!" exclaimed Mrs. Bobbin.

"Yes," said Bobbin, "promised him, without hesitating a minute."

"He's very kind," she responded, dryly.

"You can bet on that," went on Bobbin, eagerly.   "He knows who to be thankful to."

"Well, what did he promise you?" queried Mrs. Bobbin, spreading another piece of bread for little Tommy.

"Hey!" exclaimed her husband, stopping to look at her.

"Didn't he promise you anything?" said she; "you were the first to suggest him."

This seemed to be a stunner to Bobbin.   He had never thought of anything for himself.   It had never occurred to him as possible. He looked at his wife in a puzzled kind of way; run his tongue up to one side of his mouth, and then said — casting his eyes reflectively round the room — "Oh, well — I don't expect anything of that kind — you know. I don't go for a man to get an office."

"But you need it," said Mrs. Bobbin, "much more than Mr. Spiker does."

"Why, I know," replied her husband, deprecatingly, "but you know Spiker is rich and has lots of influence and all that, and, to tell the truth, my dear, he is a trifle cheeky, though it's all right enough, He spoke to Zach. about the place himself, and brought me in, as if I suggested it, and of course I couldn't say anything else, so I took it up — not that Spiker isn't a fair man, for he is."

"Well," said Mrs. Bobbin, with a sigh, "what is it all to amount to after all?"

"My dear!" said her husband with an injured air, "I did not think to hear you say that, and before the children, too. I hope the country is

something, and I hope our children may live to
know that their father thought the country was
something."

"But what has the country got to do with Zach.
Martin ?." inquired Mrs. Bobbin.

"Now, Elvira, I really wish you wouldn't,"
responded Bobbin, looking hurt. "What do you
think would become of this Republic if the Opposition should triumph ?"

"I don't know, I am sure," replied his wife.

"Ruin," said Bobbin, "blank ruin. Liberty
would be knocked down and dragged out—would
be overthrown, and your children would be beg-
gars."

"And so you are working against that?" said
Mrs. B.

"That's it," he replied. "I'm humble, it's true,
but I'm striking the bass-drum of public opinion,
as it were, with the hammer of individual sover-
eignty. I'm trying to save the country—that's
enough for me."

Now this was all very well and very laudable

in Mr. Bobbin, but his wife thought, though she did not so express herself, that it would be much better if her husband would vary his dose of liberty with bread and meat. The fact was that up to that time Bobbin had been mighty profuse with the former, but very chary of the latter. The family were chuck-full of freedom, fairly puffed out with it, so to speak, as if they had the dropsy, but while their souls were expanded with this sublime sentiment, their stomachs, unfortunately, were in state of famine, and the comparison some way made Mrs. Bobbin indifferent to patriotism, while it made her a devoted friend of family flour. She owned the little house where they lived and a quarter acre of land attached, and from this little patch of ground and her odd jobs for the neighbors came the principal support of the family. Bobbin, good-natured soul that he was, always had some big thing in contemplation, but he never quite reached it. He was always skirmishing, but never getting into an actual engagement. His wife's question rather startled him; and, although he couldn't seriously think of so great an office as the Collectorship, he began to imagine that his labors for the party certainly did deserve recognition.

"I tell you what," said the little man, "they couldn't refuse me if I asked it."

"Then ask it," responded his wife.

"But what?" queried Bobbin.

"Anything that will keep us comfortable; no matter what," returned she.

"I'll do it," said Bobbin, with wonderful energy, bringing his little fist down on to the table. "I'll tell Spiker to-morrow that he must divide."

Mrs. Bobbin looked astonished, but pleased. Such spirit was unusual with her husband. He had raised his fist again and was threatening to strike the table harder than before, when there came a knock at the door, and it left his fist poised in the air. A boy stuck his head in and said:

"Mr. Spiker wants to see you down to the office right away."

Bobbin started as if it had been a summons

from an emperor. He grabbed his hat, and saying to his wife that Spiker, no doubt, wanted to consult him about the campaign, started out.

"Get in a word for yourself, if you can," said she as he was closing the door, but the almost frightened glance that came back to her through the opening made her sorry she had said anything.

It was a consultation, and Bobbin's work was laid out for him with great particularity. A ratification meeting was to be held, and Bobbin was to put up the posters, to prepare the big wagons, to arrange the seats in the grove, to borrow the flags and the banners, to make the frames for the transparencies, and at night, when a torchlight procession was to come off, he was to carry a lamp, and see that the cheers were loud and frequent. In fact, Bobbin was to be filled with spontaneous enthusiasm on the evening in question, and was to charge the others with the same effervescing sentiment, deftly uncorking them at regular intervals to keep them from bursting.

"Zach. will be at my house when the procession

3 D

passes," said Spiker, "and it must halt in front of the porch and mass there. When I come out with him you just bawl your best licks. Tell the boys to bear down and raise the roof off."

Bobbin promised, and after the arranging of a few more details, the meeting broke up. One by one the citizens dispersed, but Bobbin lingered. He was trying to get courage to speak to Spiker about that little place, but he failed, and as usual in such cases, the longer he waited the more difficult the task became. On one pretense or another he delayed his departure, and when Spiker buttoned up his coat to leave, Bobbin stood in front of him and on either side of him, and kept saying something to prolong the interview. Finally, when Spiker walked out and up the street, Bobbin ambled along by his side saying he would walk home by way of the former's house. At the gate, Bobbin, instead of passing on, leaned against the fence with an air of deep interest in the approaching preparations, and endeavored to think of something new. Spiker passed coolly in, and

had taken a step toward the house, when Bobbin
—with a feeling of desperation began.

"Oh!" he exclaimed, "I was thinking (here
Spiker turned back and Bobbin lifted his eyes
contemplatively toward the stars, and continued—
sliding off as it were on to a switch)—about how
many seats do you think, now?"

"Oh, that's all fixed," responded Spiker; "put
up enough for five hundred; the rest can stand
up."

"Oo-hoo," said Bobbin, "that's what I was
thinking myself. And the posters?"

"Why, put up the usual number in the usual
places," said Spiker.

"Yes, that's all right," said the timid little man,
and then as Spiker turned again toward the house
Bobbin heaved a big sigh.

"Well, good night!" he exclaimed, and started
slowly on.

Spiker had got half way up the walk when
Bobbin, with a reckless bravery that amazed himself, suddenly stopped and called the great man

back to the gate, while he returned to that point
himself. He was a rod or two away when he
began saying in a trembling voice, "See here,
Spiker, if Zach.'s elected, don't you suppose I
could get something, too?"

Spiker was almost transfixed with amazement.
"What!" he exclaimed, as if he thought his ears
deceived him. "*What!*"

"There!" said Bobbin, putting his hand out as
if to ward away a blow. "It don't make a bit of
difference, of course. I just thought I'd see what
you thought."

"You!" said Spiker. "*You* have an office!
Well! Bobby! that's devilish good!"

"I was only fooling," said Bobbin, with an air
of hilarity. "Good joke, ain't it? Good night!"
and he sped away into the darkness.

But Spiker stood at the gate chuckling, and
wondering, and thinking, and when Bobbin had
reached the middle of the block he called to him.
The little man turned, and with a voice rather
choked and husky said, "What!"

"I'll think of it, Bobbin," shouted Spiker, "Maybe something can be done."

How the little man's heart bounded at these words. He grew half an inch taller in a moment, and when he reached home he awakened his wife and exclaimed triumphantly, "Well, by George, I've done it."

CHAPTER IV.

THE CAMPAIGN.

Those were busy days that succeeded the nomination of Zach. The campaign began in earnest, and was what the politicians call short, , sharp, and decisive. It was a new and pleasant experience for Zach., though not without its severe trials. At the commencement all was clear sailing, and only plaudits greeted him ; but after awhile the opposing candidate was nominated, and though not expecting to win, he made an ugly fight for it. He was a rough, but keen and experienced debater, and when Zach. was compelled to meet him he found that his path was not strewn exclusively with roses. The opposition newspapers also attacked him on every side, as only American newspapers can, and ere the campaign was over a large minority of the good people of

the Fifth District looked upon Zachariah Martin
as the impersonation of all that was wicked and
devilish. Still, as we said, there was a charm
about the situation that made the experience a
pleasant one. With the larger half of the crowds
that assembled, Zach. was the hero, the Cincinnatus
who had come forth at his country's call to save
it. It was pleasant to look down into the eager,
upturned faces, and to make those faces grow
stormy, sad, or merry at will. Sometimes also a
deeper and better feeling came over the young
speaker, and he felt, and deeply, the great responsibility that rested upon him, and the duty he
owed to the generous men who trusted him so.
implicitly. Not in a politic and self-interested
way did he feel this, counting the tenure of his
office and the cost or benefit to himself in all he
did, but in that greater sense which makes the
statesman to resolve now and then to do right,
though popular applause may turn against him,
and to stand up for truth and righteousness even
though the very persons for whom he contends,

misjudge and crucify him therefor. In these
moods Zach. grew impressive, earnest and con-
vincing, and the multitude followed him as the
Crusaders followed Peter the Hermit; but such
moments of exaltation were few, and usually Zach.
was a very good representative of the ordinary
politician. He sometimes rebelled against the
tricks and devices so often employed on the
stump, but never carried his opposition far. His
confidential advisers were men who wanted to
win, and were not very scrupulous as to the
means employed. With them sentiment was an
excellent thing on the platform, but it had no
place in the committee room, and they scouted
the virtuous givings-out of public speakers as
"springes to catch woodcocks," and the solemn
declarations of the party platform as "glittering
generalities."

I am not moralizing in this story. I am not
writing a tale with any well-defined idea of a
moral, I believe, but O! for the time when a
truer manhood shall come into our political life,

when more of our politicians shall be statesmen, and more of our statesmen patriots; when insincerity, trickery and cunning shall meet with contempt instead of reward, and the name "politician" shall be no longer a term of reproach.

Let no one scoff at this. There is need of such men. There is need of more true men in all the grades of politics, from the highest to the lowest. Holding aloof in the "I-am-holier-than-thou" sort of spirit will not answer. No American can be truly faithful to his duty as a citizen who is not in the larger and better sense of the word a politician. Bad men degrade politics by mingling actively in political affairs. Let good ones exalt by lending to it the grace and virtue of their own respectability.

Well, the campaign went on. Peggy grew strangely interested in it, and very proud of Zach. His father grew anxious and troubled, and as for his mother, the charges which flowed from the opposition newspapers against her boy almost set her frantic. When the joint debate between Zach.

3*

and his opponent came off at Hiltonville, she attended, and actually cried with rage at the cruel words of the base man, who so ridiculed and abused the pride of her heart. She could have scalped him on the spot, and might have done so had she not been restrained by wiser counsel.

"And this young man," said that distinguished speaker, "this young man, hardly escaped from the protecting wing of his mother, prattles to you about duty. *You*, gentlemen, whose heads are gray in the service, who saw the sun rise and set upon the bloody fields of Tippecanoe and Lundy's Lane; who saw the charge at Chepultepec, and the banners of the Republic waving over the halls of the Montezumas. This man prates to you of duty — a beardless boy instructing gray-haired veterans, Narcissus directing Apollo, an unfledged gosling leading the gods."

O! how the words stung, and stung Zach., too, as well as his mother, but he had got partly used to them, while all was new and terrible to her.

"You didn't give it to him half hard enough,"

said Mrs. Martin, after the speeches were over and they were on their way home. "The nasty brute, to get up there and abuse and insult me! Why didn't you pitch into *his* mother, Zach.? though I suppose if he ever had one he brought her gray hairs in sorrow to the grave long ago."

Zach. promised to lash him next time, and, after giving him some minute instructions as to just how he was to take the offender down, Mrs. Martin subsided into something like calmness.

And so the weeks went by until, finally, Zach. came home hoarse and tired, and the campaign was ended. He was very glad it was over; and took his seat by the fire with a big sigh of relief. He had little anxiety about the election, for the district gave a large majority for his party, so he could wait complacently. The second day passed and brought him the news. He was elected very triumphantly, and, as the word spread, the roll of the drum and the shouts of the villagers warned him that a call of congratulation was in contemplation.

And they came, Spiker and Bobbin and the rest. The fife shrieked, the horns tooted, and once more, for the last time Zach. fervently hoped, he heard the words of a campaign song composed in his honor, but which had grown wearily familiar to him. When the chorus rang out, however,

> Brave Zach., strong Zach.,
>   None so well as he
> Plants upon the battlements
>   The flag of liberty,

Mrs. Martin drew herself up proudly and laid her hand upon her son's shoulder with an air of supreme enjoyment. Then came hand-shaking and, inside the house, where a large part of the crowd retired, a recounting of experiences. It was singular what deference was paid to Mr. Spiker. Next to Zach. he was the lion. When he opened his mouth, which was by no means unfrequent, every other tongue was stilled. Without his saying so, the impression was out some way that the victory was directly traceable to his efforts.

Spiker was one of those big, positive characters

who go through the world elbowing everybody and stepping on men as they do on the rounds of a ladder. To dispute with him meant a scene, and as most men hate scenes, he generally traveled along in his self-asserting way unmolested. Such persons are by no means dangerous, and, when sufficient cause presents itself, always find plenty of men to oppose and vanquish them; but people do not tear down stone walls when there is an easy path around them, unless it becomes necessary. So when some one suggested a plan in Mr. Spiker's presence, and that gentleman replied in his big voice, " No, no! stuff—nonsense! it won't do at *all!*" the other party was not likely to press it, unless it was a very important and vital matter. To Bobbin, meek-eyed and timid as he was, the presence of Spiker was simply overpowering, and the idea of disputing with him was so absurd as to be entirely out of the range of his imagination. His business was to laugh when Spiker laughed, to frown when he frowned, and generally to play a sort of minor accompaniment to the major part

performed by his great exemplar. But Bobbin was
so convenient to Spiker as to be almost a necessity, and the great man had his plans for the little
·man which, as usual, were like to be successful.
Bobbin had never opened his head to Spiker about
the office since the night referred to, but he knew
by the mysterious or knowing winks bestowed
upon him now and then that the latter had not
forgotten it. To-night Bobbin watched Zach. timidly, and stood near him as if owing him an
apology for so doing, but all the time he was bask-
ing in the sunshine of Spiker's eyes, ready to look
stern when Spiker looked stern, and to draw down
his mouth when Spiker drew his down. If the
latter told a story, it was Bobbin who enjoyed it
most; and if his patron was looking at him, he
tried to grow very red in the face, and to appear
almost suffocated with the mirth he was trying to
restrain. During the evening Bobbin saw Spiker
take Zach. into a corner and talk to him earnestly,
now and then glancing to where he (Bobbin)
stood. The latter tried to look unconscious, but

he shifted around uneasily on his feet, and laughed very loud at a point made by one of the company, when, in fact, there was nothing to laugh at. Finally Spiker called, " Bobbin, come here!" Bobbin looked surprised at the summons, and tried to appear very unconscious as he approached the two gentlemen. Spiker collared him as he would a school-boy.

"I've been telling Zach.," said he, "just what you've done in this 'ere campaign! By thunder, I never saw a better worker! Now, you're as poor as a sand-hill crane. You've got half a dozen children that look as if they'd inherited a rag factory. You ought to have some way to live, and that's what I've been telling Zach. There's nothing here that I know of, but there are any quantity of places in Washington that a member of Congress can get whenever he's a mind to. Now, my plan is that Zach. get you a place there. He's agreed, and says he'll do it if he can, and I know he can. Now, that's settled. When a man does good work, by George I like to see him paid for it, and, Bobbin, you'll be paid, mind that!"

"Oh, I don't want any pay," said Bobbin, with the tears glistening in his eyes.

"Stuff!" cried Spiker, slapping him on the back. "You do want it, and you'll get it, eh, Zach.?"

"I shall surely feel delighted to help you, Bobbin," said Zach, "and as Spiker says, I presume I can. At any rate, I'll do my best, and I owe you much besides."

"That's the talk," said Spiker. "What did I tell you, Bobbin?" and slapping the little man again, Spiker wiped his face and puffed, and looked immensely placid. Promising to talk over the matter again, the subject was dropped here, and soon after the company separated. Bobbin went home in a state of bewilderment. He was wondering whether he could ever do enough to repay Spiker, and how he would act in the new and great life that seemed opening before him. And thus the campaign ended.

CHAPTER V.

IN WHICH ZACHARIAH ENTERS UPON NEW SCENES.

The engagement existing between Peggy and Zach. was not a public one. Only the family knew of it, and so the remarks of gossips did not annoy the young people. Peggy had gained a conception of what would be required of her when she came to support a part of the dignity of Zach.'s new position, and she had tried hard to qualify herself for the place — that is, she toned herself down somewhat, tried to read the various ponderous books that Zach. provided for her, and tried to learn a good many things which, under other circumstances, she would have heartily. despised. Among the books thus supplied her were several on drawing, and these had a fasci- nation for her. Though unaided, she developed in a few months a decided cleverness in sketch-

E

ing, and frequently delighted Zach. with her proficiency in this respect. With most of the other studies, however, she was at natural enmity, and do what she would she could not become interested. Perhaps Zach. expected rather too much of her. Few women would be fascinated with Mill on Political Economy, but this was one of the works that Zach. commended to her, and even urged most strongly upon her attention. Poor Peggy tugged away at it until her little brain was racked to bursting, but it was no use. The ideas and the words faded out of her memory before they were fairly lost to the eye.

"To think," said she, "that the women down there are familiar with such great books as these! I know I will seem like a fool to them, for I can not understand it," and then she would go poring over the pages again in the vain hope of remembering a passage with which she could delight Zach.

And so the time intervening between the election and Zach.'s taking his seat passed away. It had been arranged that immediately after his arrival in Washington he should secure a position for Bobbin, if possible. The collectorship for Spiker was practically in his own bestowal, so there was no question about that. The night before Zach.'s departure a company of his neighbors assembled to bid him good-bye. It was rather a merry company until about the hour for separation, when a somewhat sad tinge was given it. Some one proposed the health of Zach. in a little speech, to which he responded good-humoredly. A guest then called for the old gentleman, and the call being taken up loudly, there was nothing for Mr. Martin to do but come forward. He did this, but not blushing and stammering, as they expected. On the contrary, he was calm and possessed, and surprised them by speaking deliberately and to the point. He closed by saying: " My friends, as you all know, I am not a speaker or a politician. I look upon my son's election, however, with pride, and . am grateful to you for so generously aiding him. He has been taught to be faithful, honest, and industrious in his humble duties at home, and I pray heaven that he may prove equally so in his public career. While he does, may God in His goodness bless and spare him." The earnestness of the old man, into whose eyes the tears came fast as he spoke, dissipated the mirth which had prevailed, and the crowd pressed Zach.'s hand, with a solemn prayer for his happiness as they bade him good-bye.

The next morning the carriage stood at the door which was to carry the young statesman to the depot; the trunks and valises were aboard, and he turned to bid a farewell to his father and mother ere he started. Peggy stood by with a half-frightened look and with a presentiment in her heart that she was seeing the last of Zach. He took her and kissed her tenderly, and was turning away silently when, with a sudden impulse, she threw her arms about his neck and, looking up into his face, pale and anxious, said almost wildly: "Oh, Zach., you will not forget me, will you? Promise me you will not."

Zach. was not used to partings, and he was easily affected. He clasped her close to him, and his voice trembled as he replied:

"Forget *you*, Peggy! When I do, may heaven forget me."

He kissed her again and was gone. It all seemed very foolish to Zach. when he thought of it, and it will seem still more foolish to those who, in the ceaseless going and coming incident to modern travel, forget what last partings are; but it was a solemn thing to Peggy, and she went to her room sad, dispirited, almost despairing.

Zach.'s blues lasted him until he was seated in the cars and was whirling away toward the goal of his ambition. The ones who stay behind always have the hardest of it, but there were many things beside the mere spectacle of new sights to distract and divert Zach. Falling into a conversation with a gentleman, it soon became known to the latter that his fellow-traveler was a member of Congress, and Zach. became the center of attraction. As luck would have it —

and what a queer companion this same luck is
oftentimes — the gentleman was himself a resident
of Washington, and soon introduced himself as
Richard Marmaluke. He was accompanied by
his wife and daughter, the former a stately woman,
very elegant in her dress and manners; the latter
a most beautiful young lady, who made a very
decided impression on Zach. at first sight. The
ladies received him very graciously, and with that
nameless ease and air of good breeding which
charmed while it embarrassed the young member.
Before he met them he flattered himself that he
was pretty well posted in social as well as political affairs, but he hadn't been long in their company until he discovered that many of his expressions were uncouth and inelegant, and he found
that he, who could stand unawed in the presence
of a vast audience of his own people, felt sadly
rough and unpolished in the society of two unpretending ladies. In fact, so far as knowledge of
the polite world was concerned, Zach. was totally
ignorant, and he blushed guiltily when he was

forced to admit that he knew very little of the
theater, was unacquainted with the German, didn't
even know the meaning of the "kettle-drum," and
actually never heard an opera in his life. The
ladies made his ignorance tolerable, however, by
failing to seem surprised at it, and he found himself getting on swimmingly. For two days he
traveled in their company, and at the end of this
time was ready to swear that he had never spent
two such profitable and pleasant days in his life.
And how he was drawn toward the elegant young
lady, who had thus accidentally become his traveling companion! When he looked at her, and
reflected that she was a belle in the best society
of the capital, as he soon made up his mind she
must be, he not only felt proud of her acquaintance,
but very much satisfied with himself. He began
to think that it was no accident which had taken
him out of the sphere in which the Martins from
time immemorial had dwelt, but his own efforts
and his surpassing abilities, that had thus exalted
him. He began to think that Spiker's words were

literally true, and that Martin's Corners was about
to throw a statesman on the world who would
astound it.   And all the time he could not
help contrasting Miss Marmaluke with Peggy.
"Peggy!" some way the very name sounded so
coarse and countrified to him.

. Miss Marmaluke was a rather sharp-featured
young lady, with light hair, "frizzed," and large
blue eyes.   She had a way of languidly closing
the latter, and then opening them suddenly, as if to
dazzle her companion by leaving him in darkness
for a moment and then turning the supernatural
radiance of these orbs upon him.   Some men
would have imagined this to be the trick of a
coquette, but Zach., inexperienced soul, only
thought that something about her was excessively
bewitching and difficult to resist.   There was none
of this languor about Peggy.   Her eyes were
brown as was her hair, and they were always
merry with good humor or glistening with tears.
They never drooped in the exquisite style peculiar
to Miss Marmaluke, but always spoke, as did her

tongue, all that was in her heart. And then, Miss Marmaluke's hands! They were the slender aristocratic hands that Zach. had read about, and the gloves fitted them as if the kid out of which they were made had been ordained for this service particularly, and had walked up to the glove-maker with the measure of Miss Marmaluke's hand upon his back and had said, "Here I am, cut me up in her behalf alone." Ah, Peggy's black kids, even when she wore them, looked sadly different from these. And Miss Marmaluke's hair was arranged so gracefully! How it became her peculiar style of beauty, and how ridiculous seemed Peggy, as Zach. remembered her, with her two long braids, or with her absurd little knot stuck like a turnip on the back of her head.

The sun was setting as they entered Washington, gilding with gold the dome of the Capitol, which Zach. looked out upon with wonder and pride — wonder at its loftiness and grandeur, pride that he was one of the privileged few to

4

take possession of it. At the depot he bade his new friends adieu for the present, not without some rather warm expressions on both sides, and not until he had promised to visit them at their home early and often. Then he took a carriage and was driven to a prominent hotel. He was early on the ground, few members had arrived, and he was assigned pleasant quarters. Perhaps Zach. felt rather crest-fallen that the clerk did not recognize his name and seem impressed with his arrival, but the bell whanged away behind the counter, and the boy was told to "show the gentleman to 46," as if he were the most ordinary traveler in the world. However, Zach. was not to be cast down by this. He dressed and went to tea, then bent his steps to the Capitol, which he examined long and critically by the light of the moon, which was shining brightly on the magnificent dome of the great structure. Returning to his hotel and to his room at last he fell to thinking, and his thoughts, do what he would, were not of home or óf Peggy, but of his new friends, the

Marmalukes, and particularly of Belle, the daughter. He could not help comparing her once more
with the young ladies of his own vicinity at home,
and it was almost with pain that he thought of
Peggy again, with her simple gown and her
freckles. Would she ever attain such grace, such
a demeanor, to say nothing of such beauty? He
felt that it was impossible, and he sighed. Just
then a knock came at the door, and a servant
entered with a card. Zach. took it and read :

𝕮𝖔𝖑𝖔𝖓𝖊𝖑 𝕰𝖇𝖊𝖓𝖊𝖟𝖊𝖗 𝕭𝖆𝖗𝖓𝖈𝖆𝖘𝖙𝖑𝖊.

Immediately the young man was wide awake.
He straightened himself and bade the servant
show the visitor up. It was his first caller.

CHAPTER VI.

IN WHICH MR. BARNCASTLE JOINS THE PROCESSION.

Zach. had only time to wonder who his titled
visitor could be when there was another knock at
the door, and the servant ushered into the room a
very striking-looking personage. He was a man
of forty-five or fifty years, clean shaven, of medium
size, but slim, and dressed with a mixture of
shabbiness and elegance that puzz'ed you. Glancing at his shoes and the bottom of his breeches
you would have set him down as a frequent patron
of the debtor's prison; looking at his waistcoat
and his gold eyeglasses, you would have marked
him as a shrewd lawyer with a comfortable practice. Proceed to his shirt collar, and thence to his
hair, and you would have made up your mind that
he was a chemist, a scientist, an alchemist, perhaps,
engrossed with his studies, with time for only pass-

ing care to his personal appearance. This in repose. When he opened his mouth, however, and began to speak, you recalled all your opinions and confessed that you did not know *what* he was, but only that he was Colonel Ebenezer Barncastle.

Zach. rose as his visitor entered, and advanced a step. Mr. Barncastle paused, threw back his head, and, jerking his mouth into a smile, said —

"I beg pardon, but have I the honor of addressing the Honorable Zachariah Martin, of the Fifth District?"

"That is my name," said Zach., "and I have the honor to represent the Fifth District."

"Just so," said Mr. Barncastle, advancing and shaking hands. "You got my card, Mr. Martin?"

Zach. replied in the affirmative, and offered his visitor a chair.

"Mr. Martin," said Barncastle, again throwing back his head and smiling, "we are glad to see you among us, sir. When I say that we expect something of you beyond the ordinary level of an ordinary member, you understand me? Hay?"

"I hope I shall be able to fill the place worthily," responded Zach., modestly.

"Fill the place!" exclaimed Mr. Barncastle. "Why, sir, you will overflow it. [See Frontispiece.] We know, sir, of your innate modesty, and we know also of your unquestioned ability. Genius, Mr. Martin," here Barncastle assumed the attitude of an orator, "true genius can not be hidden under humble guise or remain unknown in desert waste. It bursts out like the sun of noon from under the morning cloud, and shines the brighter for its temporary obscuration. Try to contract it and it expands; consume it and it rises from its ashes; shatter it and it gathers new strength and comes up smiling at the last round. Genius, guardian angel of my native land, I hail thee! Hay, Mr. Martin! Right."

Mr. Barncastle wiped his forehead with an ancient red silk handkerchief and looked thoughtful

"I agree with you, Colonel," said Zach., "that true genius can not always remain in obscurity; but I fear you flatter me."

"Don't speak of it, my friend," returned Barn-castle, looking hurt, "don't speak of it. We, sir, who are used to public characters and public life, search out the true grain from among a great deal of chaff — I must say that, Mr. Martin, a great deal of chaff — and when we see a genuine kernel we know it. I called on you thus early because we know it. I want to congratulate you on the magnificent stand you have taken for liberty."

Mr. Barncastle here reached to his coat-tail and took from his pocket a newspaper, rather faded and old, and unfolded it. It proved to be the Hiltonville "Herald," and contained one of Zach.'s speeches in full.

"You see," said Barncastle, "I do not speak unadvisedly. I hold here your speech at Hilton-ville. I regard it as an effort worthy of a Clay, sir, worthy of a Clay. Forgive me, but you have never heard this passage from another's lips. Listen :

"My countrymen, behold that flag! Look upon the white and blue and crimson banner of our country! Shall it be polluted? Shall those stripes be soiled? Shall the stars that now gleam so brilliantly be dimmed by the sacrilegious hand of the opposition? Methinks I hear a million voices respond in one thundering no, and there is rejoicing in heaven over the honor and patriotism of my countrymen."

Mr. Barncastle's voice faltered as he closed, and he turned away and took out his handkerchief to blow his nose. Zach. thought the extract rather neat himself, but he was somewhat surprised to see how it affected his new-found friend. However, he felt pleased and flattered.

"I call that," said Barncastle, turning to him, "a sentiment worthy of a Jackson, and expressed in the sublime language of a Webster. We have need of more such fearless advocates, sir — more of them! In these days, sir, we want men with sediment in them."

"I fear you make too much of my little effort,"

said Zach., "but I tell you frankly, I do intend, for one, to speak plainly and, if possible, to the point."

"And that's what delights us, sir," responded Barncastle. "We see too much of mediocrity in the counsels of the nations. It delights us to be able to say to one like you, 'Welcome among us.'"

"You have been a great deal in public life, I see, Colonel," said Zach.

"Always, my friend, always," returned the Colonel, with a matter-of-fact air."

"Closely connected with the government, no doubt?" inquired Zach.

"Intimately, intimately," responded Barncastle. "As Senator Brookhaven was saying to me this morning, 'Colonel,' says he, 'what you don't know about public life ain't worth knowing,' but I always pardon Brookhaven, he is such an old friend, you know."

Zach. felt a sort of awe creep over him. So here was an intimate friend of the great Brookhaven, whom he had worshipped for years, and

4*   F

Barncastle spoke of him as if his acquaintance was the most ordinary thing imaginable.

"May I ask what position you now hold?" inquired Zach., respectfully.

"Officially none," replied Barncastle, "unofficially a dozen. I was half a mind to go into active service again at the President's solicitation, but I said to myself, ' Barncastle, you old dog, if you want to serve the country, remain outside; be untrammeled but be vigilant.' 'Colonel,' said the President to me, 'Will you never let me put you in a place where your experience and knowledge can be of service to the country?' 'Mr. President,' I answered, ' Now, I am your friend; socially and politically your friend. No one accuses me of selfish or ulterior motives in visiting you; but were I in your Cabinet all my acts would be misconstrued. So,' says I, sliding off into verse,

> ' Let statesmen die and principles decay,
>   But give the gray-haired veteran his way.'

What I want, Mr. Martin, is the consciousness here

in this breast (Mr. Barncastle struck his stomach by mistake) of doing my whole duty. I ask no more. You understand?"

"I see," said Zach., "you are undoubtedly correct."

"Of course," said Barncastle. "The party wants advisers. · I give it my counsel. The managers say: 'We want success. We must have success. What shall we do to obtain it?' I answer: 'Organize! organize,' Mr. Martin! The Alpha and Omega, the beginning and the end, the top and the bottom sardine, I may say, of successful politics, is organization."

"Most true," said Zach., admiringly.

"Hey! That's it," said Barncastle, drawing back and looking at Zach. and smiling triumphantly. "But I must be going. The Secretary of State gives a little supper to-night, and no amount of begging would let me off. Mr. Martin, your hand." Barncastle rose and extended his palm graciously.

"I am sorry," said Zach., "that you can not keep me company a little longer, but of course I

can not detain you under the circumstances. I am
very grateful to you and hope you will not forget
me."

"Forget you, Mr. Martin," exclaimed Barncastle. "Never! You have my confidence; know
me better. You will find us straightforward, generous, whole-souled fellows to our friends, but the
very devil to our enemies. Good-night! and let
your motto be, Integrity, the keystone of the arch."
He shook Zach.'s hand once more warmly and was
gone. The latter turned back gratified, delighted.

"The high road to success seems open," said
he, "and a coach-and-four to drive me over it.
Here I am received by the intimate friend of the
President, from whom I have had words of praise
that make my cheeks burn. Was there ever so
lucky a mortal?" He had got thus far when there
was a knock at the door, and, opening it, there
stood Barncastle again, smiling, but looking
terribly perplexed.

"Pardon me, Mr. Martin," said he, "but a most
unlucky thing has occurred. Here I have just

fallen in with Admiral Griggs, who is suddenly called to New York, and will likely be dashed away on a cruise without a penny in his pocket. Banks all closed. Train leaves in fifteen minutes. Could you accommodate me with, say fifty dollars in exchange for my check on the First National?"

The idea of a trick never so much as occurred to Zach. It took almost every cent about him, but he readily answered: "Certainly, with the greatest pleasure. Never mind the check, Colonel, your word is all that is necessary."

But Barncastle did mind. "Forgive me, Mr. Martin," he said; "but there you're wrong. Business is one thing, friendship another. I always do these things by rule. There you are!" he continued, handing Zach. the check. "Many thanks."

"I believe you have the correct theory about everything," said Zach.

"The result of experience," said Barncastle, stuffing Zach.'s bills into his pocket. Then he smiled and again extended his hand. "Once more," said he, "I almost feel as if you were an old and valued friend. I shall not say good-bye to you hereafter, but only *au revoir.*" And once more he was gone.

The next day Zach. presented his great friend's check at the bank, and the teller chuckled and handed it back. Zach. blushed and stammered. The teller chuckled more than ever and winked at the statesman.

" What's the matter?" whispered Zach.

" No funds," whispered the teller.

Zach. looked at the check and then at the officer.

" Ain't it good?" he inquired.

"Oh!" exclaimed the teller. "Why old Barncastle never had a cent in a bank in his life."

Zach. slipped the check into his pocket, pulled his hat down over his eyes, and marched quietly out of the building.

CHAPTER VII.

BOBBIN GETS AN APPOINTMENT.

Zach. did not tell any one about his little experience with Colonel Ebenezer Barncastle, though to tell the truth it deeply mortified and vexed him. He disliked to be taken in so easily, and more, if possible, to lose the pride and pleasure which the compliments of Barncastle had given him. The result of his experience with that gentleman was to make him unduly suspicious, and the way he eyed strangers who sought his acquaintance thereafter, and questioned them as to their business pursuits, was very comical.

Zach. did not fail to improve his acquaintance with the Marmalukes. He visited them the second day after his arrival, and found them even more affable and gracious than ever. They were nicely domiciled in the west end of the city, and

though by no means gorgeous in their surroundings, were elegant and extremely hospitable. They
had a circle of very fashionable friends, and it was
not many weeks before Zach. began to feel quite at
home in their house.   In the meantime the session had opened and the young man had begun
his duties.   He was surprised at the seeming dis-
order which prevailed in the House, and found
that, though he might be a great man in Pine
County, he had small chance to make a reputation
here.   Some one always seemed to be before him,
and it was months before he could get the floor
even for a dozen words.   And he was equally
astonished at the kind of work which was
required of him.   He had possessed a vague
sort of notion that the duty of a member of
Congress was to rise gracefully in his seat and
proceed to speak great words upon great questions. He found instead that this was about the
last thing that such an official was called upon,
or even permitted, to do.   And he had no more
than become fairly settled in his seat before letters

from his constituents, and it seemed from everybody else's constituents, began to pour in upon
him. These letters were upon every imaginable
subject. All creation appeared to have business
in Washington which Zach. was expected to do,
and do instanter. It would be wearisome to
recount even a part of the commissions intrusted
to him, but the young man soon found that the
position he had obtained was no sinecure. Then
came the demands for office. It seemed to Zach.
that every man who had voted for him wanted to
be appointed to a position of trust and profit. He
was besieged also by those from his State who
were already occupying situations in the government service at the Capitol. These all wanted
better places, and generally preferred appointments
in the States or Territories. It struck Zach. as
somewhat singular that his constituents at Washington all wanted to get away from there, while
his constituents at home all wanted to come to
Washington.

He got along with it as best he could, but so

far had only succeeded in getting Spiker and Bobbin appointed, the former collector, the latter to a
one thousand two hundred dollar clerkship in the
Treasury.   He sent out the latter appointment
three months after his arrival in the capital, and in
due time it was received at Martin's Corners.

Bobbin was not in the habit of receiving letters, and when he held in his hand a thick envelope
bearing his name, and just above it the words
"House of Representatives, U. S. A.," it someway
made the little man faint.   He did not open the
letter then.   He put it in his pocket and started
home, determined to read it first in the presence
of his wife.   As he neared his house, however, he
suddenly felt that he ought to be prepared for its
contents before trusting himself in the presence
of his family, and so he turned off up the road.
He wanted to find a quiet, secluded place, but
someway the whole country seemed alive.   He
had a notion of getting over the fence into the
woods, but he wondered what people would think
if they saw him prowling in there without any

apparent reason, and he turned away. He got into a field on his left, and went over a little knoll into a ravine, but up on the other side he saw a man at work, and he made a circle and came back into the road. He was inclined then to read it there, but he was afraid some one would come along and see him and inquire about it; so he turned his steps once more toward the house. This time he passed round the dwelling to the stable and threw the wild and frowsy looking cow there an armful of hay. Then he looked out in various directions, drew the door shut, and pulled the letter from his pocket. He opened it and glanced at the signature, as if to make sure that it was really from Zach., then he read a sentence, and finally the whole letter, which was short but important. It informed him that he had been appointed to a position in the Treasury Department, and directed him to come on at once.

For a moment Bobbin felt like kneeling down and thanking heaven for his good fortune. It seemed to him like a special interposition of

Divine Providence in his behalf. Then came
other thoughts. He was to leave home — something he had never done before. He was to
leave his family, temporarily at least, and this
struck him as a most terrible trial. All in all, he
felt that he had suddenly become of immense
importance to mankind, and while he gladly
assumed the honors and the burdens heaped
upon him he could not help feeling a regret,
after all, that the past was dead, and a new life
was opened to him. Bobbin secretly wondered
whether he would have a title in his new position, and whether he would be an Honorable as
well as Zach.

That night there was excitement in the house
of Bobbin. It extended and widened, too, until it
embraced all the near neighbors, and one by one
they dropped in to congratulate the little man,
and talk the thing over. Zach. had told him to
show the letter to Spiker, and Bobbin had visited
the former's house and had a long conversation
with that gentleman.

"Now you are all right," said Spiker. "*Now* go ahead. You've got a chance to make something at last, and if you don't, it is your fault, that's all."

Mrs. Bobbin was delighted. She was perfectly willing to spare her husband for the promised $1,200 a year (a sum that seemed absolutely fabulous to her), especially until she could join him in the great capital, as she expected to do.

The next morning preparations were made for his departure. The village tailor was called upon to fit out the little man in a brand-new and "fashionable" suit of clothes, and he informed Bobbin and his wife confidentially that he had been in Washington during the war, and knew exactly the cut that was *en vogue* in that center of civilization. Bobbin was measured, a proceeding entirely new to him, and before the next morning the wonderful suit was cut and in process of being basted together. The whole village lent their advice to Bobbin in the emergency. He was trying to fit his little head into a felt hat, when one of his friends declared that this was folly and little better than suicide. In Washington no one that pretended to be anybody at all ever wore anything but a silk hat — a "plug," as the gentleman expressed it.

"Look at the President, when he came through Hiltonville last Summer," said he. "You didn't see him with a soft hat on *his* head."

Everybody remarked that that was so, and although Bobbin modestly responded that he was not exactly the President, "you know," "nor anywhere near it," he finally resolved, by universal advice, to order a "plug" from Hiltonville, and did so.

Perhaps the astounding appearance of Mr. Bobbin when he finally got into that new suit, and surmounted it with that tall hat, was never before presented to mortal man. Someway he looked so raw and mismatched, so to speak. The coat was too big, that was tolerably plain; but it was the trowsers that startled the beholder, and seemed to stun Bobbin. Those garments seemed determined to crawl all over his feet, and work themselves up in the mud under his shoes. They were doubled up in wrinkles, upheaved into great billows, collapsed into frightful ravines, and when the wind blew them out straight against Bobbin's thin little legs, he resembled a small schooner capsized, but with the shrouds still clinging to the masts. People remarked that they were too big, but Sims the tailor only closed his lips in a sort of pitying contempt at their ignorance. "Of course they're too big for such a town as this," said he, "but how are they for a large city? What do you know about Washington styles? Look here!" and Sims would point to a fashion-plate on his smoky walls, aged and venerable, in which were a pair of breeches that looked wonderfully like Bobbin's in some respects, and silenced all cavil by this conclusive demonstration of his artistic taste.

Bobbin bade his wife and children good - by with a sob. It seemed as though his heart was going to choke him, as he kissed them all round and passed out of the little door. Spiker was going to town, and Bobbin was to ride with him, and he got into the buggy with a feeling that this was the last of earth. Then Spiker cracked his whip, and the little fellow was whirled away, trying to smile good-bys at the faces that witnessed his departure.

An hour after, they were descending the winding road that led into Hiltonville, and Bobbin was actually smoking a cigar, and, in spite of his trowsers, looking like a genuine man of the world.

When Spiker bade Bobbin good - by at the depot, his last words indicated a prior conversation on some business between them, for he said:

"Now, remember what I've told you. If everything goes right this ain't the last thing you'll get through me, and if anything turns up let me know at once. You just stand by me straight, and you may be sure your bread will be always buttered, and buttered right." And then he squeezed Bobbin's hand and Bobbin squeezed back with all his might — the bell rung, the locomotive whistled sharply, and he was off.

It was the gray dawn of morning when Bobbin, tired, dirty, and fearfully mussed up, arrived in Washington. The dust had settled in the wrinkles of those wonderful trowsers and clung there tenaciously. His new hat had received many a rub the wrong way, and seemed obstinately resolved to defy all efforts to smooth it out. His beard had grown bristly and rough, and altogether he presented a melancholy appearance. No one noticed him, however; no one, indeed, had noticed him since the time he left home. He was absolutely hungry for a talk, and gazed eagerly out the windows as the cars entered the depot, hoping that by some lucky accident Zach. would be on hand to meet him. But he looked in vain. He knew no one, and he got out and walked aimlessly along in the crowd of hurrying passengers to the depot entrance. Here a great crowd of hackmen, expressmen, and hotel-runners were assembled, yelling at the top of their

5   G

voices, and grabbing every one they thought it safe to seize upon. Bobbin was fortunately secured by a very decent fellow who represented a small hotel close by, and the two, taking hold of the little man's trunk, carried it in a very sensible, and, to Bobbin, very proper, way to the house designated. Washed, brushed, and fed, our friend began to feel like himself again. The house was near the Capitol, and, having rested, he set out about two o'clock in the afternoon to explore that immense pile and find Zach. He had inquired at the hotel for the latter, and was amazed to find that the people there did not know, and had not even heard of, the great statesman. Bobbin sauntered along toward the west entrance to the Capitol Grounds, and when he reached the gate stopped and looked timidly in. Groups of people were passing in and out, and finally he ventured to walk up the broad way himself. He reached the front of the Capitol and halted. He was not sure that he had not committed trespass already in entering the grounds, and he did not like to offend further by going into the building. Seeing a gentleman coming down the steps alone he accosted him and inquired if he could go inside. The man looked at him a minute, smiled, and said : "Of course you can;" and so Bobbin went on. Arriving in the rotunda he was lost again; but after a while was directed toward the hall of the "House," and walked straight ahead until he was stopped by a tall man, with full whiskers, who stood before a couple of green doors.

"That way," said the official, jerking his head back, and indicating the way to the gallery, "unless you want to see somebody."

"I want to see Zach. Martin," said Mr. Bobbin.

"Send in your card," replied the man.

Bobbin looked at him silently, not comprehending exactly what he meant; but seeing a man come up, take a blank card, write something on it, and tell the big-whiskered man to give it to "Collins," Bobbin divined the state of things and asked for a card himself. The official handed him one, and taking it to a window near by Bobbin wrote on it, very plain:

For Mr. Zach. Martin.

Zach.. 1 want to see you.   I'm out here in the hall.

TIMOTHY BOBBIN.

This he handed to the official, and that gentleman disappeared with it.   Presently he returned and handed the card back.   Mr. Martin was not in.   Bobbin felt disappointed, but he looked around, and, seeing the crowd ascending a stairway, he joined them, and presently found himself in the gallery of the House, looking down upon that buzzing, bustling, unruly assemblage known as the House of Representatives.

For a while he forgot everything else in looking at the strange scene.   Away off on the other side a man was talking at the top of his voice, no one appearing to pay the least attention to him, while every now and then the presiding officer would hammer away on his desk with a little mallet and shout something that no one seemed to understand. Bobbin was sure the desk would be broken into splinters by the terrific pounding, and, innocent soul that he was, concluded that this was a sort of noon recess, and that the boys were eating their dinner and having some fun. He waited curiously, therefore, to see the House called to order and business begin.

He was sitting close to the railing which divided the ladies' from the gentlemen's gallery, and all at once his attention was attracted by hearing a voice close to him that sounded strangely familiar. He looked, and almost within reach he discovered Zach. bending over a seat in front of him in which were two ladies. The ladies were richly dressed, and were gayly chatting with Zach., who appeared oblivious to every other sight or sound. Bobbin's first impulse was to call out, but he restrained himself, and watched anxiously for his friend to recognize him. But the latter never once glanced his way. It was a full hour before the Martin's Corners statesman got up and started out. He had ascended the gallery steps only part way when Bobbin coming close to the railing, called out:

"Zach.! How d'ye do?"

Zach. turned and looked at Bobbin closely before he recognized him, then walking up to the railing, pleasantly held out his hand. Poor little Bobbin seized it in both his own and fairly hugged it, while almost bursting out crying. It seemed that all home was there in the presence of Zach., and for a moment he could say nothing, and made no reply to the latter's question as to when he arrived.

Calming down after a little, his companion took him out into the hall, and accompanied him through the Capitol. It was a comical sight to see Bobbin, with those extraordinary trowsers turned up at the bottom to keep them from getting under his heels, and his silk hat, a size too large, pulled down over his ears, treading along at Zach.'s side, his face all smiles, and his eyes glistening with pleasure as they took in the many wonders of that vast pile. Vulgar people stopped now and then to stare at Bobbin, but he never suspected the cause of their attention. Once Zach. stopped to speak to a gentleman whom he met in the corridor, and after shaking hands introduced Bobbin. The latter also shook hands with the gentleman, and then stood by while he spoke a few words to Zach. on political subjects. Finally the gentleman passed on, nodding pleasantly as he turned away, and saying "Good day, Mr. Bobbin, glad to have met you."

"Does he look as you thought he did?" inquired Zach., as the stranger disappeared.

"Well," said Bobbin, "I don't know as I ever thought much about it. Who is he?"

"Who is that?" exclaimed Zach.; "why, that is the great Marcus Aurelius Tompkins, of Massachusetts."

Bobbin liked to have fallen flat. He turned to look at the back of the great man disappearing in the far corridor, and faintly ejaculated:

"*That! he* Tompkins?"

"Yes," replied Zach.

"Good Lord!" exclaimed Bobbin.

"Didn't you understand the name?" inquired Zach.

"No," exclaimed Bobbin, with a long breath. "And do you know *him* ?"

"Certainly," responded Zach., "and so do you."

"Zach.," said Bobbin, solemnly, "I never thought I should shake hands with a man like that."

Zach. smiled.

"And he spoke to me and called me by name when he went away, just like anybody," said Bobbin.

"Exactly," returned Zach., laughing.

Bobbin pulled his hat down a little lower, gave his trowsers a hitch upward, and pursued his way thoughtfully. As they returned toward the House side, they met the two ladies to whom Bobbin had seen Zach. speaking in the gallery. They smiled very sweetly, and Zach. colored as he smiled in return. They stopped him for a word or two

and Bobbin waited; but Zach. did not introduce him.

Th   night Bobbin wrote a long letter home,
in which he dwelt on his cordial reception by
Zach. and his meeting with the great Tompkins.
"I tell you what," he wrote, "my heart began to
bob when I found out who it was, but, upon my
soul, you wouldn't have been surprised if you had
seen him in front of the store at Martin's Corners;
so easy-like and natural."

After this Bobbin went to bed, and slept well
for the first time in nearly a week.

5*

CHAPTER VIII.

ZACH. GOES INTO SOCIETY.

The Marmaluke mansion was ablaze with lights, and servants in swallow-tailed coats and ornamented with button-hole bouquets ushered in the throng of guests. The drawing-room was pretty well filled, and in the rear-parlor a couple were holding a very animated conversation. The first was Mrs. Barker, a woman of forty, perhaps, large and fine looking, but with a worldly, what one might call a fleshly, look that was not altogether pleasing to the physiognomist. She was elegantly dressed, and had that careless ease which denotes one accustomed to fine apparel and seemingly above it. She was waving a fan, which she now and then closed to tap her companion with, enforcing a remark in this way, and then opening it again with that peculiar grace which women know how to employ so well. The person talking to her was a young man of perhaps twenty-four, a small, slim, gentleman, with a little tuft of blonde whiskers on his chin, a diamond stud in his shirt-bosom, and a brilliant ring upon his little finger. He had a very lamb-like face, and his clothes seemed to have grown upon him as a lamb's fleece covers that type of animal inno-cence. This was Mr. Henry Audley, or Mr. G. Henry Audley, as he was wont to subscribe him-self, a very wealthy young gentleman, son of a widow, devout and respectable, who divided her time between New York, Washington, and her son. Audley was the intimate friend of all the ladies, especially the middle-aged ones, by whom he was constantly made useful and to whom he confided all his secrets. He had a weakness to be considered a regular masher of female hearts and a very wicked young man with the fair sex generally, but there was not a well-authenticated instance of his ever having broken a heart in his

life, nor likely to be one.   Just now he was telling
Mrs. Barker a little bit of scandal.

"It was the strangest thing," said he. "Five
elopements and one marriage."

"Oh, no! not five," said Mrs. Barker.

"'Pon my honor," ejaculated Audley.   "Now,
I'll tell you.   First she ran away with her music-
teacher."

"That's one."

"She left him," said the young man, "because
he wouldn't play 'Ever of thee' on the flute.
Then she eloped with a tailor."

"That's two," said Mrs. Barker.

"Then she ran off with her father's coachman."

"That's three."

"Then she left with a California gambler, and
now she's married a bank-teller.   She tried to
elope with that little Japanese Minister, but some
friends put him on his guard.   They say she has a
splendid figure."

"Oh, I warrant!" said Mrs. B.

"Wears one-and-a-half shoes."

"Nonsense!" said Mrs. Barker.

"Fact!" said Audley, energetically. "I know her shoemaker. He told me so himself. I'm going to get an introduction."

"For shame, Audley," said a voice behind them, and a lady — Mrs. Sampson, a woman with a pale-faced husband who was rarely seen away from home — joined the group. "You are a very naughty man — isn't he, Mrs. Barker?"

"I hope after making her acquaintance he will avoid us," replied Mrs. Barker.

"Oh, no, confound it!" said the young man, "I wouldn't speak to her, you know, if you think I had better not."

All this was about a rather fast and fascinating young lady who was just then the talk of the town.

"That's a good boy," said Mrs. Sampson, and she playfully patted his head, while he smiled like a child commended for not stealing fruit-cake.

The trio were here joined by Commodore

Grimshaw, a gruff, hearty old naval officer, who had been placed on the retired list because of a wound which disabled him from active service. When told of the proposition of Audley, and of the manner in which it was received, Grimshaw grunted out a decided "Humph."

"Why not make her acquaintance?" said he. "What's the matter with her? You women are so easily horrified, and there ain't one in twenty of you that wouldn't elope fifty times in fifty hours if you had the opportunity."

"Ah," said Mrs. Marmaluke, who had joined the group, "the Commodore will have his jokes, you know."

Here Grimshaw turned around to grasp an old gentleman by the hand, and Mrs. Marmaluke had her attention called to a new arrival.

"The Commodore will have his jokes," said Mrs. Barker, repeating the words of Mrs. Marmaluke. "Yes, and his sprees, too, I am informed. Did you hear of his performance on the avenue after the banquet last Tuesday at the Arlington?

It was too funny. They say the police actually had
to carry him home."

"Mrs. Marmaluke always apologizes for him,"
replied Mrs. Sampson. "Of course I don't know
anything about it, but they say she and the Commodore were a little too friendly for Mr. Marmaluke's peace of mind a few years ago."

"Good gracious!" exclaimed Mrs. Barker.
"Well, I'd like to know what she found in him.
He looks like an inverted iron-clad."

"Hush!" exclaimed Mrs. Sampson, "here comes
that woman-killer of the capital, Mr. Hartwell."

The person named, a black-eyed, black-whis-
kered, and rather *distingue* gentleman of thirty or
thereabouts, came forward with Miss Belle Marmaluke and her mother, and joined the group.

"You know Mrs. Barker and Mrs. Sampson, of
course?" said Mrs. Marmaluke, turning to Hartwell.

"It ought to make a man smile at every misfortune to be able to say that he has that pleasure,"
returned the latter, bowing gracefully to the ladies.

"Now, that's really fine," said Mrs. Barker. "Where do you get all these beautiful compliments, Mr. Hartwell?"

"Ask yourself, madam," returned that gentleman. "If I am inspired, the source lies hereabout. I am as dumb as an oyster when out of your company."

"You all know that Mr. Hartwell never flatters," said Belle.

"Oh, never!" chimed in Mrs. Sampson.

"I would, I confess," said he; "but where's the necessity?"

"You didn't flatter that beautiful creature you had at the opera Wednesday," said Mrs. Barker.

"With the curls?" said Mrs. Sampsen.

"And the last year's bonnet," said Mrs. Barker.

"Do tell me who it was," put in Belle.

"Oh, a mere passing acquaintance," answered Hartwell.

"A passing acquaintance, and have her at the opera!" said Mrs. Sampson. "*Now*, Mr. Hartwell!"

"Oh, I did not take her!" said he. Then, as looks of incredulity met him, he continued: "'Pon my honor, now. Saw her there with a friend, and took his place by her for half hour."

Just here there was a little bustle at the entrance, and Commodore Grimshaw appeared, with a lady on one arm and Mr. Zach. Martin on the other. Mrs. Marmaluke and Belle hastened to meet them.

"There is the great statesman, the Hon. Zachariah," said Mrs. Sampson.

"Mercy, what a name," exclaimed Mrs. Barker.

"The name is a Scriptural one," said Audley, who had rejoined the group.

"Indeed!" returned Mrs. Barker. "Who was the original or Scriptural Zachariah?"

"I don't know exactly," said Audley, "but he had something to do with cattle and chickens and one thing and another."

"And our friend Mr. Martin was named Zachariah because he was old Zachariah's successor, I suppose," said Mrs. Barker.

H

"Yes; fact," answered Audley; "I heard them say that Martin used to plow and drive oxen, and do all that sort o' thing, you know."

Mrs. Sampson here nudged Mrs. Barker, and directed her attention to the new comers.

"Do see Mrs. Gammill and the Commodore," she exclaimed. "Did you ever see a more deceitful woman?"

"She's working for an invitation to the naval ball," answered Mrs. Barker.

"Wouldn't she and old Grimshaw cut a handsome figure on the floor?" laughed Mrs. Sampson.

"She has a pretty necklace, there," observed Hartwell.

"And nearly broke poor Gammill up getting it," returned Mrs. Barker; "so I am informed."

Zach., Mrs. Marmaluke, Belle, Mrs. Gammill, and the Commodore here approached and shook hands. While Zach. was being introduced to one or two of the party whom he had not met before, Mrs. Barker kissed Mrs. Gammill very affectionately.

"I never saw you looking so well, my dear," she exclaimed.

"And Mrs. Gammill might return that compliment, I am sure," said Zach., extending his hand to Mrs. Barker. "What an interesting party you always draw around you! What do you say to make them so merry?"

"We were putting Mr. Audley through his catechism just now," said Mrs. Barker. "It's wonderful the knowledge he has of Scripture and ancient history."

"What was the question?" inquired Zach.

"Why, these were the questions propounded by Mrs. Sampson and myself. She said: 'Audley, give your attention, hold up your head, and take your hands out of your pockets. Who is the first person mentioned as having spoken in Scripture?'

"Audley—'The whale.'

"'To whom did the whale speak?

"Audley—'To Moses in the bulrushes.'

"'What did the whale say?'

"Audley—'Thou art the man.'

"'What did Moses reply?'

"Audley—'Almost thou persuaded me to be a Christian.'

"'What did the whale then do?'

"Audley—'He rushed violently down a steep hill into the sea, and perished in the waters.'"

A loud laugh greeted this rather old, rather profane, but rather clever sally, and no one appeared to enjoy the satire on Audley's proverbial stupidity more than that young gentleman himself. "Bravo, bravo," cried the crowd that had collected about Mrs. Barker, and there was a great clapping of hands; but Commodore Grimshaw did not appear to relish the joke. "Oh! these women!" exclaimed that salty veteran. "That was done to cover up some of her backbiting, but I almost feel like forgiving the woman for her ready tongue."

At this juncture music was heard in the grand drawing-room, and the party made a movement toward that point.

Zach. and Mr. Hartwell approached Belle at

the same moment, and each offered an arm. Belle hesitated, and then placing her hand on Zach.'s arm said, smiling to Hartwell :

" I believe Mr. Martin was first," and gracefully sailed out of the room.

" First!" repeated Hartwell, gazing after them, and smiling bitterly. " Yes. *He* is an Honorable. Let him improve the time while he is, for his honors may not last forever. They shall not, if I can help it."

" Come, Mr. Hartwell," said Mrs. Barker, appealing to the young man, " I am dying for company."

" With all my heart," replied Hartwell, offering his arm.

" Not all," said Mrs. Barker, looking up at him.

" Yes, all," said Hartwell, smilingly.

" Except that borne away by the Hon. Zachariah," returned Mrs. Barker. Hartwell laughed, showing his even white teeth close together, and then bit his lip as he walked away.

Mr. Audley and Mrs. Sampson were the only persons left behind. During the above conversation Audley had been industriously offering his arm to half a dozen ladies, each of whom had unluckily provided herself with an escort just as he came to hand.   Not at all discouraged, the young man turned to Mrs. Sampson, and, bowing very low, said: "Mrs. Sampson, may I?" and Mrs. Sampson returned the bow with a most graceful inclination, and answered: "You may."

The dancing and the flirting and the gossip were going on swimmingly in the drawing-room when a couple of middle-aged gentlemen entered the hall and stepped from there into the library at the left.   The younger of the gentlemen, who came in as if at home, was, in truth, the master of the house, Mr. Marmaluke, and his companion was a local judge of some repute, named Spalding.   They took off their overcoats and threw them carelessly over the chairs, while Mr. Marmaluke looked out through the open doors at the scene in the parlors.

"There they go," said he, drawing off his gloves. "The Commodore and my wife, Audley and Mrs. Sampson, and——"

"Martin and your daughter," put in the Judge. "Fine fellow that Martin, Marmaluke. I'd encourage him."

"He *is* a rising young man," replied Marmaluke.

"Yes, yes," responded the Judge. "Got a fine legal brain, too. When the bill was up last week to encourage the judiciary by an increase of salary he saw through it like a chief justice. 'If we want fine legal ability,' said he, 'we must pay better prices for it.' And so we must."

"Not that we haven't fine legal ability now, Judge?"

"By no means. But can we keep it? That's the question."

"You are not going to resign, I hope?" said Marmaluke, solemnly.

"I ought to," returned Judge Spalding.

"But you won't," said Marmaluke. "You see it's not so bad after all. We plain citizens may make a little more money, but we run a good deal more risk, and have no honors showered upon us. If we get attention we have to pay for it, while

you officials have cannons fired, and military drawn
up, and carriages furnished, and the hospitalities
of the city tendered every time you go out.   You
ought to be willing to slice a little off on the salary.   But here," proceeded Marmaluke, going to a
side-board and bringing out a decanter and glasses,
"Robertson County.   The best; arrived last night.
If anything can soothe the ruffled spirit of the
judiciary, it's such whisky as this.   Let's try it."
The Judge tasted it, lifted his eyes in mute appreciation, and then swallowed the remainder at a
gulp.

"Now for a smoke," said Marmaluke, and the
two gentlemen went up stairs, where the odor of
their cigars would not disturb the guests.

Zach. and Belle had danced twice, and then, a
little tired and heated, they stepped across the
hall, and entered the library.   They were conversing very rapidly, and Belle seemed vastly pleased
and interested.   Zach. had been telling her of his
home, and was much pleased at the apparent enjoyment she manifested.

"And you lived there all your life?" she inquired.

"All my life," returned Zach., "worked on the farm summers and went to school a mile through the snow in winter."

"Dear me!" exclaimed Belle.

"Oh, it was not so bad," said Zach.

"But had you no amusements?" she inquired.

"Nothing but spelling-schools," returned Zach., "and occasional parties at a neighbor's, seven or eight miles away. Then came the sleigh rides. Ah, there *was* real enjoyment. You know nothing about them here."

"I have had them in New York," replied Belle.

"Yes; but those are poor affairs," said Zach. 'Some way the snow looks tired, and there is none of that roughness and abandon which lends it such a charm in the country. You want a sleigh twenty feet long, filled with boys and girls and buffalo robes. Then four horses loaded down with bells — not flat, spiritless little tinkling bells, but all kinds, from the deepest bass to the sharp-

6

est treble.   Away we go down the road and round
the turn, the old woods echoing the merry jingle,
the horses arching their necks and dashing
along—

> "Keeping time, time, time,
>   In a sort of runic rhyme,
>   To the tintinnabulation that so musically wells   ·
>   From the mingling and the jingling of the bells."

Zach., growing interested in his description,
and remembering the many incidents that he had
enjoyed, was almost carried away, and stopped
short as he recovered himself and begged pardon.

"Pardon!" said Belle, with her eyes glowing.
"Why, it is excellent.   I don't wonder you are
called an oràtor.   I am sure you deserve to be."

"You flatter me," said Zach.

"Not a bit," returned Belle.   "I am certain you
deserve it."

"And do you like the appellation?" said he,
placing his hand upon hers as it rested upon his
arm.

"Indeed I do," she returned.   "If I were a

man it seems to me my highest ambition would be to sway a crowd, and by the force of my eloquence make them obedient."

" My father always ridiculed this power," said Zach. " He never believed in it. He is always talking of quiet and contentment and domestic peace — peace in a cottage, or rather in a farm-house, which amounts to the same thing."

"But how must domestic peace be sacrificed in a palace more than a hovel?" said Belle.

"The very question I asked him," responded Zach., "but he is very old-fashioned and very singular in some of his notions, and Peggy always sided with him."

"Peggy?" exclaimed Miss Marmaluke, curiously.

Zach. blushed, and Belle noticed it, and this made her twice as curious.

"Who is Peggy?" she inquired.

" Have I never told you?" said Zach.

"No," replied Belle ; "is she your sister?"

" No."

"Oh, your sweetheart?" said she. "Now, don't deny it."

"Not now," said Zach., with an effort, and looking mean as he made the denial. "We used to be rather tender with each other a long time ago."

Ah, was it then so long since that tender parting, and did Peggy indeed seem so far away to him?

"She is an orphan — Peggy Clover, by name," he resumed, "who was brought up in our family. A noble girl," continued Zach., resolutely, and determined to make some sort of amends for the cowardice which made him deny her. "A noble girl, honest, sincere, and one who, if she had only had advantages, no man would be ashamed of; but of course she is perfectly ignorant of the world, and for that matter of accomplishments."

"And one with your discernment and tastes," said Belle, artfully, "must have a companion as well as a help-meet."

Someway these words seemed so true to Zach. And again came up that mental contrast between the eloquent girl at his side and plain Peggy, with her simple, sober dress, her tanned face and hands, and her hoydenish manners.

"I was mad to think of marrying her," he said to himself; "mad to think of it. It is not too late to save both Peggy and myself from the misery of an unequal union."

Belle seemed to read his thoughts, and to encourage him in putting that absurd first love aside.

"No," said Zach, turning to her and resuming. "My ideal is this. I would have the honor and gratitude of my countrymen. I would have a faithful, a beautiful, a loving, and an intellectual wife. I would have wealth, of course, a house in town, a cottage in the country, where quiet would only be dearer for the contrast with the bustle of fashionable life; and then, Miss Marmaluke, it strikes me my earthly happiness would be complete."

Zach. unconsciously drew Belle nearer to him as he spoke, and she, nothing loth, hung more tenderly on his arm.

"And with such a man," said she quickly, and then recovering — "a man who could command such miracles, I mean — what woman would not be happy?"

"And you would?" said Zach. softly, bending down to her.

"Yes," replied Belle, "with even far less than this."

"With what less?" said he.

"All," she responded. "All, I think, save the frank generous heart that could wish for such things for my sake."

"And who would not wish for them and win them, too, for one like you?" said Zach., passionately. "At least who would not be armed and girded for the work with you to cheer and strengthen him? What obstacle could prevent our realizing the ideal if we went hand in hand together? Miss Marmaluke! Belle!" ——

A rustle was heard at the door, and they both looked around. Hartwell was sauntering by and looking in. His white teeth shone through his black beard as he smiled cynically and passed on.

The sight seemed to recall some thought to Belle, for she straightened up and said hurriedly: "Let us return. Our absence will be remarked. I hear some one coming now." She turned as she spoke, and Zach., rather disappointed, started forward with her. At the door he paused and said: "And when shall we continue the conversation?"

"To-morrow," said Belle, hastily, and they passed into the drawing-room.

Hartwell was standing at the library door a few minutes after, when Mr. Marmaluke and the Judge, having finished their cigars, came down stairs.

"Hello! Hartwell!" said Marmaluke. "Enjoying yourself alone, eh? and you such a beau. For shame! What has become of your gallantry?"

"Only a step out here for a breath of fresh air," responded Hartwell. "I am just returning."

"That's right," responded Marmaluke. "Give

the ladies the pleasure of your society while you are young and good-looking. When you are as old as the Judge and myself they won't notice you."

"I shall endeavor to improve the time, sir," said Hartwell, showing his white teeth again and passing into the parlor.

"A nice young man enough," said Marmaluke, looking after him. "Would be somebody, probably, if he would leave this energy-destroying city and go out into the world. By the way, Judge, a young man ought never to hold office. It unfits him for everything else and makes a sort of helpless imbecile of him. Offices, at least all the good ones, ought to descend like incense on old codgers like you and me."

"Now, Marmaluke," said Judge Spalding, "you don't understand these matters. As I was saying when you broke me off, the judiciary is the palladium of our liberties. Without an incorruptible judiciary what is a country worth? How can it be incorruptible when its stomach is continually craving turkey and lobster salad, which it is too poor to buy? What does Blackstone say? Governments are — "

"There, now, don't," interrupted Marmaluke. "Don't get on to Blackstone. The prisoner pleads guilty to every count. What is the sentence?"

The Judge glanced wishfully at the magic side-board. "The court is silenced," said he, "and assesses the fine at two more toddies, and it must be paid without being replevied."

"Good," said Marmaluke, and he proceeded to pay the fine.

At the other end of the hall at this instant a curious scene was being enacted. Belle, accompanied by Hartwell, was standing there, while he, in low, but almost fierce tones, was addressing her.

"I heard it all," said he. "The fool would have proposed and you would have accepted, for what I know, if it had not been for the noise I made."

"And what can I do?" she replied. "You know I am acting the part under instructions."

"You are of age, I believe," said he.

6*   I

"Yes, and my own mistress; but what then? Shall I disobey my mother? What have you to offer me? Show me a home where you can take me."

"You know I can not do this now," he responded; "but let us marry and trust to reconciliation."

"Oh, I have seen too many such cases," she replied. "My mother is ambitious. She wants position. She thinks she sees in Martin a lucky genius, who will rise to the highest places. If I were to marry you she would supply my place here with some relative, and the house of Marmaluke is not rich enough to support two such luxuries."

"And what do you propose to do?" he said.

"I really do not know," she replied.

"You will not marry him?"

"No, I suppose not."

"But if he urges you?"

"I will accept him."

"Accept him!" Hartwell's face darkened, and

he clenched his hands nervously. "Take care, Belle," said he.

"Oh, it is easy enough," said she, quickly, "ma will not object to delay. It will give her time to see if her predictions prove true, and to look out for more eligible parties."

"And how long can this last?"

"How long do you want it to last?" said she.

"I want time to better my own condition and to look after his," replied he. "One, two, three years, if necessary."

"It can be done," said Belle.

"In that time," continued Hartwell, "I will put obstacles in Mr. Martin's way that will dispel your mother's fancy, and you must help me."

"I!" exclaimed Belle. "What can I do?"

"Opportunities will offer. You must recommend me to him — to his confidence."

"I don't see how this can help you," said Belle.

"Never mind; do it," he replied. "Put it strong; urge it as a special personal favor. If he cares for you, he will not refuse you anything. I know them all." .

"I will do what I can," said Belle, "trust me for that. Now let us go in,—and for mercy's sake don't look like a volcano if I happen to speak to the man again."

Hartwell, whose countenance had grown placid, smiled once more and proved his recovery by immediately going up to Zach., and entering into a very pleasant conversation, in which Belle soon joined.

"Where have you been, you wicked men, all the evening?" said Mrs. Barker, a few moments after, as Judge Spalding and Mr. Marmaluke entered the room.

"There, you dear creature,' said Mr. Marma- luke, familiarly; "the Judge and I have had a serious case to consider."

"Yes, madam," said the Judge, "an alleged vio- lation of the revenue laws."

"No doubt," responded Mrs. Barker; "from the

odor in the library I should say a brewery had been seized and the contents confiscated."

"Your woman's instinct is right," replied Mr. Marmaluke; "it was a brewery."

"But the man was innocent," said the Judge; "I would have sworn that the moment I smelt his handiwork."

"And on tasting it," continued Marmaluke, "the man was triumphantly acquitted."

Audley, who had stood by hearing this raillery, here broke into an immoderate fit of laughter. "I see!" he exclaimed, "I see! By Jove! That's good! That's rich!"

"Why, stop the man," exclaimed Mrs. Barker. "He'll suffocate himself"

"Some one pound him on the back," suggested Mrs. Sampson.

"Oh, give him time," said Marmaluke. "He's not used to such wit; he'll recover soon."

"It reminds me, you know," said Audley, catching his breath and trying to speak distinctly, "it reminds me of a story of a judge."

"Certainly," said Mrs. Barker, solemnly.   "It reminds him of a story of a judge. How strange!"

"You are sure it was a judge, Audley?" said Marmaluke.

"Oh, yes," replied the young man, tittering.   "He got drunk and stole six silver spoons."

"Oh, no!" exclaimed Mrs. Barker.

"Come now, young man," said Judge Spalding, "that won't do."

"Upon my honor," said Audley, looking serious; "by mistake, you know."

"Oh!" said Mrs. Marmaluke; "Oh!" exclaimed Marmaluke; "Oh!" echoed the rest.

"Yes," continued Audley; "and he found them in his pocket next morning just before a deuced fellow was brought before him for stealing a pig. 'Guilty or not guilty,' said the Judge, or the lawyer, or some of them. 'Guilty, but drunk,' pleaded the thief. 'Where did you get your liquor?' inquired the Judge. 'At Miller's,' responded the man. 'Release the prisoner,' roared the Judge. 'Let him go! That whisky of Miller's would make a thief of the Angel Gabriel,' and so the fellow got clear."

At the termination of his story, Audley burst into an uncontrollable fit of laughter again, the others remaining very solemn and serious.

"Marmaluke," said Judge Spalding, "our young friend can't have been meddling with your Robinson County liquid, can he?"

"Impossible!" replied Marmaluke.

"Strange," continued the former, "that keenness like that should inhabit such tender youth. He deserves something of his country. Let's remove him to the jury room."

"Ladies, excuse us a moment," said Marmaluke; "we want to reward genius and invigorate innocence. Audley, this way," and taking the young man by the arm the two gentlemen escorted him to the library.

"Our friend, the Judge, has a little too much this evening," remarked Mrs. Sampson, as the gentlemen disappeared.

"Never mind," responded Mrs. Barker, "he can't drink more than Marmaluke."

While this scene was transpiring at one end of the room, Zach. and Belle were improving the time at the other. It was quite late, and he was making ready to go.

"I hope your evening has been pleasant," said Belle.

"My evenings are always pleasant when I spend them here," he replied.

"Oh, thank you," said Belle; "will you come to-morrow?"

"With pleasure."

"I have a favor to ask of you," said Belle, remembering her promise to Hartwell.

"You have only to name it," said Zach.

"You are so kind," returned Belle, looking up at him gratefully. "I shall see you to-morrow."

"Yes, and, let me hope, alone," said Zach.

"Alone," echoed Belle, bowing; and then, pressing her hand, Zach. took his leave.

That night he sat in his room until way into the morning, thinking of his new life and the strange change that had come over him. When at last he fell asleep he dreamed that he was at the farm again. Peggy had her arms about his neck, and was saying, once more, beseechingly, "You will *not* forget me, Zach.?" and he was responding, while a new sun rose in the east and bewildered and maddened him, "When I forget you, Peggy, may Heaven forget me."

CHAPTER IX.

MR. BARNCASTLE AGAIN.

Zach. had seen Mr. Barncastle many times since
that gentleman so quietly relieved him of the fifty
dollars on the night of his arrival in Washington.
At first he felt like seizing the rascally dissembler
by the throat and compelling him to refund, but
he overcame this desire and permitted his polished
admirer to pursue his way in peace.   Further than
that the surpassing assurance of the man rather
commanded his admiration.   Unlike most debtors,
Barncastle was by no means disposed to shun those
he owed.   Indeed, he took pains to seek them out,
and, after apologizing briefly for his shortcomings,
enter into a political discussion with the ease and
ardor of an old and accomplished statesman.   So
fair were his promises, so seemingly sincere his
regret at his inability to refund the sum borrowed

of Zach., that the latter was at first very much mollified over his loss, and was inclined to believe that the enemies of Barncastle had slandered him; but the proof became so strong in a short time that he was compelled to place that gentleman as first in the list of all the chronic borrowers he had ever known.

As before stated, it was the custom of Barncastle to seek out his creditors wherever he could find them, and begin a well-worn and oft-repeated apology. He seemed to delight in this almost as much as in obtaining a loan in the first place; and to those who had lent him, he became an absolute terror. They would slide around back ways, slip out at side doors, turn up cross streets, and take roundabout cuts through alleys and unfrequented places to avoid him. There was something excessively comic in this reversal of customary practices, and Barncastle could truthfully proclaim himself lord of the avenue. And it must be said that he did not hesitate at times to make capital out of this terrorism.

"There comes Senator Touchstone," he would say to a chance acquaintance, looking ahead of him. "Now watch him and I will show you a piece of ingratitude." A moment after, the unfortunate statesman, observing Barncastle approaching him with that smile of resolute complacency, would dodge up a street, or in at a convenient shop-door, and Barncastle would nudge his companion with an air of "I told you so." Before they parted that companion would hold the impression that the honorable gentleman who had displayed such trepidation was Barncastle's debtor, ashamed or afraid to look the latter in the face. He would likely learn to his cost the real truth before many days, however, from practical experience, and so no great harm was done to senatorial reputation.

Barncastle's constant apologies and excuses to Zach. at last grew excessively tiresome. Some way that gentleman always took pains to introduce the subject just at the time Zach. most desired to avoid it. Meeting the latter in the crowded reading-

room at the hotel, Barncastle would dart forward
with a glad smile of recognition, and, extending
his hand, remark:

"Why, Mr. Martin! This *is* a pleasure, a great
pleasure; yet it is embarrassing. I really did not
expect to meet you to-night, and neglected to
bring that little amount with me. Will you please
say where you will be at 1:45 to-morrow, and let
me settle the matter? 'Pon my word, it worries
me;" and Zach. time after time had replied that it
was of no consequence; it could be handed in at Mr.
Barncastle's convenience, conscious at the time that
various persons in the room were winking and
smiling at the scene, and glad to stop Barncastle's
mouth at any price. The latter, however, turned
these interviews to profit. Comparative strangers
who were thrown into Zach.'s society, seeing him
recognize Barncastle, observing him conversing
with him, or going to one side with him, as he
frequently did to prevent the man from publishing
his greenness to the whole room, were led to
regard the former as a man of some importance,

an opinion which Mr. Barncastle did not hesitate
to take advantage of at the very first opportunity.
He had a way, too, of sauntering through the
hotel, and seeing Zach. engaged in conversation
passing quite near, lifting his hat, bowing, and
making some appropriate remark, as much as to
say, " We great men must recognize each other."
There was none of your false humility or self-
abasement about Barncastle.   He never spoke to
Zach. that he did not seem to say, " It was a lucky
thing for you, young man, when you made my
acquaintance."   .

Finally Zach. found himself, like the others we
have mentioned, dodging corners and slipping out
side doors to avoid Barncastle ; and at last this
persecution became unbearable.   One day as he
was turning a street corner he came face to face
with his evil genius, and there was no way to
escape the meeting.   Barncastle began as usual.
" Martin !" exclaimed he, grasping the latter with
one hand while he slapped him familiarly on the
back with the other, " I owe you fifty dollars."

"Well," returned Zach.

"Well,' repeated Barncastle; "no, sir, it is not well;, it is extremely ill, but I have just given the last cent I had to the three infant daughters of a deceased classmate."

"Yes," replied Zach., "the same story."

"No," said Barncastle, "I beg your pardon. The last time, if I recollect right, it was the family of an organ-grinder."

"It does not matter who it was," said Zach.; "you didn't have the money then, and you haven't got it now."

"You've hit it exactly," said Barncastle.

"Then what are you stopping me for?" said Zach.

"To express my sorrow, my mortification," returned Barncastle, bowing very low.

"The devil take your sorrow and mortification," said Zach. hotly. "I don't want to be stopped half a dozen times a day by a debtor, and hounded to death, to be informed that he can't pay me."

"Mr. Martin," said Barncastle, reproachfully,

"this is cruel — it is, I may remark, ungrateful.
Suppose you have a friend; his name may be
Smith or Perkins — it don't matter about that —
but you dote on him, your heart yearns for him.
In an evil hour —"

Zach. would hear no more. He brushed past
Mr. Barncastle and left that gentleman talking
wildly to the air, but when he got a quarter of a
block away he could hear the latter repeating the
names of "Smith or Perkins, as the case may be,"
hurling them and the moral he wished to incul-
cate at Zach.'s retreating form with great spirit
and persistency. After that, however, Barncastle
only troubled the young statesman at long intervals.

CHAPTER X.

THE BEGINNING OF TROUBLE.

Bobbin did not see much of Zach. for a few days after his arrival, and time hung pretty heavily, as he had not yet begun work. He had made some acquaintances, however, of a rather peculiar character, and these now and then afforded him a good deal of amusement. A circus and menagerie was exhibiting a few blocks away, and the "dashing equestriennes," the "daring gymnast," the "india-rubber man," the "old clown," the "East India snake entrancer," and other wonderful men and women were quartered at the hotel. Bobbin listened to the talk of these persons, and heard their astounding stories with great interest. He could hardly believe, as he saw and heard them, that they were the same persons he was accustomed to behold in the ring, and it took two

7   K

or three visits to the circus before he was able to convince himself of this fact.

The snake entrancer was a peculiar object of wonder to Bobbin.

One night this personage, after eyeing Bobbin very closely at intervals, came up to him and, tapping him mysteriously on the shoulder, said, in an undertone:

"Goin' into the Treasury, eh?"

"Yes," returned Bobbin.

The snake charmer shook his head and looked still more mysterious.

"Been examined yet?" inquired the man.

"No," said Bobbin. The fact is, the latter never knew until his arrival that he was compelled to undergo an examination, and, although not a bad scholar, he felt considerable alarm over the fact.

"Humbug!" said the snake charmer.

Bobbin did not answer.

"Know what they're going to ask you?" queried the man.

"No," said Bobbin.

" Tricks," said he.

" How tricks ? " inquired Bobbin.

" Catches," said the snake charmer, and then he went on to tell Bobbin how they fooled a friend of his who went before them. He told the little man so much that Bobbin resolved to be on his guard, and so was not taken by surprise when the following questions were propounded to him by the Civil Service Board, before which he appeared on the very next day:

1. Which is right:
"The house is being built," or "the house is building? "
"The ship is being sailed," or "the ship is sailing? "
"The horse is being eaten," or "the horse is eating? " .
"The book is being read," or " the book is reading? "
"The fiddle is being played," or "the fiddle is playing? "
"The boy is going," or " the boy is being gone? "

2. How many Hessians did the British bring over here during the Revolution?

3. If it takes a cork one inch in diameter at the top, three-quarters of an inch at the bottom, and three inches long to fill the neck of a demijohn, how many corks of the same size would it take to fill a chasm one and 63-1000 miles broad at the top, and sloping irregularly to the bottom, which is 4-10 of a mile in width, with a hole in the center 100 feet deep?

Bobbin was given fifteen minutes to answer
these questions. At the end of that time he
replied to the first of the series without any
regard to the rule of their analogy, but according
to the dictates of common sense. In regard to
the Hessians he stumbled. This was one of the
things of which the snake charmer had not
warned him, but he submitted a reply so novel
that it took immensely with the patriotic board.
He said:

"I can not answer definitely as to how many
Hessians the British brought over, but they
brought over a good many more than they took
back."

In reply to the mathematical problem he boldly
took the advice of the snake entrancer, and
answered that it could not be solved. So Bobbin,
after being chafed and frowned upon, and made
the subject of grave nods and wise shakes of the
head, passed the examination, and was allowed to
enter upon his duties.

When the circus broke up, and struck its tents,

and loaded its performers, Bobbin stood beside a big wagon which had the snake entrancer and his wonderful wife perched on top, and bade them good-by with real regret. And he waved his hat to them until they were out of sight, and he was once more alone.

*   *   *   *   *   *

And how was Peggy thriving all this time? A peep into the home of the Martins will reveal this. It was the first of March, and Zach. had been gone between three or four months. At first his letters had been frequent, and his descriptions of Washington life minute and interesting. He had told them of the Marmalukes, and though a twinge of jealousy seized Peggy at some of Zach.'s enthusiastic praise of Belle, she never doubted his loyalty, and dismissed her fears before they had time to assume a definite shape. He had sent her many books — books of poems, books of fashion, books of etiquette, books of art, but, with the exception of the latter, she only studied them because it was Zach.'s wish, this.

being law to her.   On the day, or rather evening, in question, Peggy was diligently engaged in reading a work on etiquette, which Zach. had particularly recommended to her.   She sat by the lamp in the "front room" at the Martins and read and re-read the passages, which someway refused to find a lodgment in her rebellious head.   Finally she came to the following passage :

"Every lady should cultivate her style of walking.   A graceful carriage is absolutely requisite to a refined deportment.   The walk should not be too stiff, neither too careless.   An elastic, gliding movement is the most genteel, and can be easily attained by a little practice."

"An elastic, gliding movement," repeated Peggy. "That seems easy enough.   It is something like this, I suppose — a kind of g-l-i-d-i-n-g movement," and she skimmed across the floor with the book in her hand.

She was practicing this new movement, greatly to her satisfaction, when Mr. Martin entered.

"Why, what on earth is the matter with you

Peggy?" said he, looking at her in amazement.
"What are you capering round in that way for?"

Peggy ran up to him, blushing and laughing,
and threw her arms round his neck.

"Oh, ho! you watched me, did you?" she
exclaimed. "Well, now, I'll tell you. I'm 'qualifying;'—that's what Zach. calls it—qualifying
myself for high life."

"Humph!" grunted the old gentleman.

"See what the book says," continued she. "'An
elastic, gliding movement is the most genteel, and
can be easily attained with a little practice.' There,
didn't I tell you?"

Mr. Martin stroked his nose and looked at her
thoughtfully.

"I believe that boy has run mad, Peggy," he
said. "Now whoever saw a gracefuller curt'sy than
you can drop when you try? As for style, there
never was a better one, and now that blockhead
wants you to change it, and go bending yourself
double and getting your back up and your spine
twisted by his new-fangled way of doing things.

You've got to go and make yourself crooked where nature made you straight, and straight where she made you crooked. But I wouldn't do it, not if twenty Zachs. wanted me to. I'd keep my little body straight as an arrow and supple as a sapling, in spite of all of 'em."

"Now, you old sweet thing," said Peggy, patting his cheeks, "you are old fashioned, and I like you for it; but then Zach. knows what they'll want down there among the Chinese, and Rooshans, and all the big folks, better than you do. So here I go for the style." And Peggy spread her skirts out and walked across the room in high glee.

"Now look at that," said the old gentleman. "Why, I suppose they'll make you put yourself in some kind of a horrid shape when you dance, too, won't they?"

"Oh, yes," replied Peggy, "they're very particular about that. Zach. says I must be just as stiff as a mackerel. He says I must about half walk and half dance, and be very careful not to hop up."

"Not to hop *up!*" exclaimed the old gentleman. Why, what *is* dancing at all, but hopping up?"

"Well," said Peggy, slightly puzzled, "this is slow dancing — s-l-o-w, you know," and she dwelt on the word as if to make its meaning perfectly plain.

"Yes, I should say it was slow," responded he. "Now, do you know, Peggy, if you was to go before the President and dance natural, you would charm his heart right out of him. Dance the Opereel, for instance. Ah, there was a dance for you!"

"The way we danced it at the big party when Zach. first went away to school?" said Peggy, brightening with the recollection. "Wasn't it splendid?"

"It's been a good while," said the old gentleman, "since I danced, but it seems to me those old tunes are the best of all. They make a fellow dance whether he knows how or not. I remember how the fiddler could make me jump when he began that time — I couldn't keep still a minute —

7*

Rum de doodle-doodle dum tum, doodle doodle," and Mr. Martin began humming an old air with great spirit, while Peggy, suiting the action to the word, gayly balanced down the center of the room. As she came back the temptation was too strong, and the old gentleman joined in, the two cutting about as lively a figure as could well be imagined. While they were in the very midst of it, the door opened and Mrs. Martin put her astounded head into the room.

For a moment that lady seemed speechless with amazement. Then she pressed her lips together, walked in, and shutting the door, put her back against it.

" Well," she exclaimed, with a great breath, looking severely at her husband, " if you ain't a-getting lively in your old age then I don't know. And *you* a deacon of the church. You oughter be ashamed o' yourself. And to be leadin' Peggy off into them old dances, too. I don't know what Zachariah *would* say. There's the books that he sent her and she don't know a word of 'em, but she must go hazing around the room and tittering and you a-leadin' off in it. I declare, Joe, I *would* be ashamed."

"We just commenced as you came in," said Peggy, appealingly, and it was those very books of Zach.'s that brought us into it, wasn't it?" and she looked toward her late partner. "Now, I'll show you," continued Peggy, noting the look of incredulity on Mrs. Martin's countenance. "There! it was this," and Peggy got the book and read, "'A graceful carriage is absolutely requisite to a refined deportment.'"

"Carriage means your gait," interrupted Mr. Martin from the corner, where he sat holding his chin in his hands, and perspiring very freely.

The old lady only scowled at him contemptuously, and Peggy went on.

"'The walk should neither be too stiff nor too careless. An elastic, gliding movement is the most genteel, and can easily be attained by a little practice.'"

"There!" said Peggy, "I was showing Father

Martin how well I could do it, and then we got to talking about it, and then — then —"

"Then you went to galloping round, you and the old man, like a couple of spring calves," interrupted Mrs. Martin. "Let me see that book." Peggy handed her the volume, and the old lady read the passage marked out for her. "Let's see you do it," said she.

"Walk?" inquired Peggy.

"Yes, walk," replied Mrs. M.

Peggy went across the floor in a very graceful way, until she got close to the old gentleman, when she caught his eye, and the two broke out in a loud laugh, ending in a bound and a stumble by Peggy which landed her on the floor at the old gentleman's side.

"Oh, *do* giggle," said Mrs. Martin, testily. "You care a good deal for what Zach. wants, don't you?"

"Well, don't I do it right?" said Peggy, wiping her eyes.

"No," responded Mrs. Martin; "you don't do it at all. An e–e–e" ("elastic," suggested Peggy "elastic, gliding moment," said Mrs. Martin, "is something like this"—and the old lady threw her head on one side, elevated her chin, and walked across the room, while old Mr. Martin indulged in a loud guffaw.

"Well, laugh!" she exclaimed, "laugh as much as you please, but I know that's about the way."

"It's a mighty poor way, then," said he. "Now, Betty, don't you think this style o' dancing and walking is thunderin' nonsense?"

"No, I don't," said Mrs. Martin. "If Zachariah says it's right, it's right, that's all."

"Of course," he replied, "that's the way they do down there, but our old way was much better. Don't I remember how I used to see you tripping along, as straight as a pine and as nimble as a deer, jumping fences and running races like an Indian princess? That was a sight for you; it was worth a big sum to look at you."

Mr. Martin spoke enthusiastically, and his wife grew mollified.

"And the dances we used to have," he went

on ; "and the figure you used to cut, with half the county crazy over you."

"Oh," interrupted Mrs. Martin.   "You mean those balls down at Smith's Corners?"

"Every-where, every-where," continued the old gentleman, waxing eloquent ; "every-where you went, no matter where, let Joe Martin and Betsy Kelly lead off,' said the fiddler; and away we went in the Virginia reel, or the monnymusk, the envy of the whole room."

"Or the French four," suggested Mrs. Martin, thoughtfully.

"Yes, that was another good one," said Mr. Martin. "Let me see, how did that go? 'Forward two?'"

'No," said Mrs. Martin, now thoroughly interested. "Let me see; this was the tune." And the old lady hummed the air of that ancient figure in a sprightly manner.

"That's it," exclaimed Mr. Martin ; "then came the forward two!" He looked inquiring and doubtful, and his wife stopped humming the tune to explain. "You begin here," said she, extending her hand, which he clasped, "then when the tune struck up we went off in this style."

Mrs. Martin again began the tune, and, inspired by old recollections, forgot her late explosion, and for five minutes there was balancing, swinging, capering down the center, approaches, retreats, and some grand displays of genuine old-fashioned dancing, such as the home of the Martins had not witnessed for years. At last, out of breath, and ashamed of having yielded in this manner, Mrs. Martin dashed out of the room and off to her own chamber. When Mr. Martin sought her, a half hour later, she was in bed, and answered an inquiry of his by saying, "Don't talk to me; you've got me into a pretty scrape to-night."

And Mr. Martin, like all good husbands, obeyed the injunction, and did not talk.

And so the days ran along until the last of the month. Peggy was making headway with her studies, and looking anxiously forward to the time when Zach. would again be with them.

It was a pleasant evening on the day named when an incident occurred to Peggy that changes the entire course of this story, as it changed the entire course of her life.

The day's work was done, and the evening sun was setting unusually bright and warm. The waters of the little lake reflected the expiring rays, which seemed to linger there, loath to bid the world good-night. Peggy sat at her window intently engaged in fastening the pretty scene before her on a bit of canvas, when John, a laborer about the farm, came in and handed her a letter. It was from Zach., and she clasped it close, while she laid aside her brush and canvas. Then seating herself by the window, she opened and read it. As she did so a look of dead surprise came over her. This gave place to pain, and then to a grief which was pitiable in its extremity. When she finally finished the letter she crumpled it in her hands, bowed her head upon it, and flooded it with an agony of tears.

But she never stirred. An hour passed, and

the twilight deepened into darkness, yet it found her there. An hour later still, and they discovered the poor girl and asked her the cause of her grief. She handed the letter to them without a word, and only bowed her head again.

L

CHAPTER XI.

IN WHICH PEGGY BECOMES A WANDERER.

"I tell you, don't talk to me," said old Mr. Martin to his wife the morning after the receipt of the unwelcome letter alluded to. "I say it's a scurvy, disgraceful trick in any man, let him be my son or anybody else."

"Now, Joe," responded Mrs. Martin, "you know very well that Peggy was not a match for Zachariah. Of course she'll do for our boys here, and make a good wife for any of them, but it's natural that Zach. should look higher."

"Look higher!" exclaimed Mr. Martin, with a tone of utter contempt and impatience. "Why didn't he think of that before? Must he break the poor child's heart before he thinks of looking higher? The scoundrel!"

"Why, highty-tighty," responded Mrs. Martin;

"you act as if that girl was more to you than your own son."

"My son is so much to me," replied the old man, "that I hate to see him beaten in good sense and manliness by a woman, and Peggy does it."

"Why, what more could the boy do, I wonder?" said she. "Don't he tell her he will always be her friend, and try to show her that his position in life ain't suited to hers?"

"You, a woman," replied the old gentleman, "and talk like that? I've never been a woman, but I know enough about the tribe to know that the biggest insult any man can offer one is to coolly tell her that, although from his exalted position she can not be his wife, yet he will kindly condescend to be her friend. Any girl with the spirit of a mouse would die before she would accept such an offer."

"Oh, you know a great deal about women!" responded Mrs. Martin.

"I know a plaguey sight more than I used to,"

said the old man, warmly. "*You* needn't throw my
ignorance in my face after profiting by it."

"Oh!" exclaimed Mrs. Martin, tossing her head.

"Well, 'Oh,'" repeated the old gentleman. " I
tell you Zach. Martin has done a disgraceful act,
and I shall take pains to speak my mind to him as
well as to you. A man that will have his head.
turned and his soul puffed up by a little good luck
ain't fit to be the husband of an honest girl, that's
the truth. If you don't like that just put it in
your pipe and smoke it," and with this Mr. Martin
walked out of the room and slammed the door
behind him.

It will have been seen from the foregoing that
Zach. had at last broken his engagement with
Peggy, and the letter was the bearer of these tid-
ings. It required a great effort on his part to
write it, but he had accomplished the task at last,
and was glad when it was over. He expected a
storm over it. He supposed that Peggy would
pout and his father scold, but he believed that ere
his return home the affair would blow over and

he could resume amicable relations with Peggy
without difficulty. Zach. was about as verdant in
matters of the heart as in knowledge of men, and
he was as much mistaken in his transaction with
Peggy as he was in that with Barncastle.

When Mr. Martin slammed the door behind
him and went out, after his tilt with his wife, he
passed around to the house toward the road,
intending to visit a neighbor. As he reached the
front gate, however, he saw Peggy seated on the
steps, and he stopped. Peggy was not crying.
She had passed beyond that now. She sat with
her elbows on her knees and her hands to her
face, looking away off across the fields to the blue
woods beyond, very thoughtful, very sad. She
smiled faintly when she saw Mr. Martin, and he
halted with the gate half open, closed it, and came
and sat down by her.

"I wouldn't mind it, Peggy," said he. "He's
not worth it."

She choked a little at this. "I don't care," said
she, "he wanted me to study, he wanted me to

be quiet and dignified and ladylike, and I did try to be. I didn't do anything I wanted to. And now!" She stopped, afraid to trust herself further.

"I wouldn't mind it at all," repeated the old gentleman, soothingly, "it will be all right yet."

"It's the great ladies who have done it," continued Peggy. "Oh, that's what it is. He's fallen in love with one of them, and will marry her, of course. But to think, Father Martin, that he could write *that* to me." Here Peggy took Zach.'s letter from her pocket and read the following passage:

"You know, Peggy, we'll be just as good friends as ever, and if you should marry one of these days I promise you a gift that shall make your eyes sparkle."

"To think of that," said she; "he thinks I have no heart; that I have no feeling; that I can marry any one."

"There my child," said Mr. Martin, stroking her head with his broad palm, "you will be righted one of these days, never fear."

"It hurts my pride so, you know," said Peggy, looking up to him mournfully.

"I know it; I know all about," replied he. "It hardly hurts you worse, Peggy, than it does me."

He said this so tenderly, that she felt like throwing herself on her knees before him in gratitude for all his kindness.

"You have always been *so* good to me," she said, taking his hand in both hers, and holding it tight: "so good."

"Do you know," she continued, after awhile, "there was a paper in the letter which I did not understand; I think he put it in by mistake. Look at it," and Peggy took a small folded paper from the envelope and handed it to Mr. Martin. The latter took it and read it aloud. It was a receipt, and ran thus:

THE NANTUCKET INSURANCE COMPANY,
$7,000.   OFFICE OF THE GENERAL AGENT,
               Washington, D. C., Feb. 12, 18—.

Received of Zachariah Martin seven thousand dollars, being for seventy shares of stock in the Nantucket Insurance Company, the same to be delivered to said Martin at this office within thirty days from the date hereof.

[Signed.]   RICHARD HARTWELL, Secretary.

" Seven thousand dollars," mused Mr. Martin. I think, Peggy, this has something to do with money I sent Zach., but I told him to invest that in government bonds.   He's so crazy he has put this in your letter without noticing it.   Never mind, it's not important.   Keep it, Peggy, and if he ever wants it let him come to you for it."

She put it back in the letter and looked thoughtfully on the ground.   "He'll never come to me for that or anything else," she said.   "He's given me up for good.   It will be the last thing between us."   She did not say this bitterly, but with a simple sadness, touching and full of pathos.

"And a pretty trick it was," exclaimed Mr. Martin, growing excited once more.   "But I knew what it would all come to.   Now, Peggy, what did you do for that boy?   Didn't you read all them books he sent you?"

"Every one," replied Peggy.

"'The love of woman surpasseth knowledge,'" said he; "and what else, now?"

" I learned music, and studied French, and then

you know I tried to paint!"—She stopped abruptly, and, laying her hand on his arm, said, " I've a notion to show you something, though I thought I would keep it secret till Zach. came home. I will;" and Peggy got up and went into the house. Presently she returned with a piece of canvas, on which was a portrait. Mr. Martin started when he looked at it. 'Twas a picture of Zach., capitally executed, as natural as life.

"Heavens and earth!" exclaimed Mr. Martin, " If it ain't Zach.! Did you make this, *you*, Peggy?"

"Yes," said she, her eyes filling with tears; "but I never could have done it if I hadn't loved him so much."

"And this is the girl," said the old gentleman, holding the picture to one side, and distributing his attention between Peggy and the portrait, "whom that numskull forsakes because she is ignorant. He was ashamed of you, wasn't he, Peggy; *ashamed* of you?"

"Yes," murmured Peggy.

"Why, confound my eyes," said he; "when I
8

was in Philadelphia I saw likenesses not as good as that which cost a good five hundred dollars. The boy is a fool. He takes after his mother. You're enough sight too good for him. He don't deserve you, Peggy ; and mind, now, if I can ever be of any service to you, ask me any day for money, or friendship, or anything I have, and it is yours and welcome. Dry your eyes and let me see a smile on your face once more. It will do my old heart good, indeed it will."

And Peggy put her arm 'round the neck of that truest of all friends, and tried her best to smile for his sake.

Peggy thought much after this of her future, and what she would do. One thing kept running forever in her head. It was the statement of Mr. Martin that portraits, no better than that of Zach., were sold in Philadelphia. But, alas, Philadelphia was the unknown country to her. She asked herself how many thousand miles it was to that city, and could not realize that modern improvements in travel had almost placed it at the door.

"What if I am somebody, after all?" she said to herself one night, sitting in her old place by the window. "What if it only needs thought and work to make me the equal of those he admires. What was it I read last night?" Peggy reached and took up a book and turned over its pages hastily. She stopped when she came to this passage:

"Half our great men and women have been developed through some startling circumstance that roused their best energies, but which was looked upon at the time as a calamity."

Peggy re-read this passage, and then closed the book and leaned back thoughtfully. "What if it should be so with me?" she said to herself. "But I forget. What could there be in poor ignorant Peggy. And yet the portrait! Five hundred dollars, he said, for a poorer picture than that—in Philadelphia. But I ain't in Philadelphia, and have no chance of being!"

She sat long and silent, turning the matter over in her mind. When she finally moved it was with a sudden determination. She stood straight up, full of resolution and courage. "I'll go," she said. "I'll go to Philadelphia! I can work there as well as here. If I stay the women will laugh at, and the men will pity me. There, no one will know who or what I am, or inquire what broke my heart. I *can not* stay here. Anywhere, anywhere, but in the place where I have lost his love and am so miserable."

Before Peggy closed her eyes that night she had matured her plans. She dared not tell Mr. Martin of them, confident that he would interpose objections that she could not overcome, and though her heart rebelled against leaving one who had shown her such kindness and sympathy without asking his advice and receiving his blessing, she dared not do it. She had a little money, enough to carry her on her journey and support her humbly for a time, and she knew she had but to ask Mr. Martin for more to be very well provided for such a trip, and to be in a condition to retrace her steps if this should become necessary. She learned that a train passed a little station five miles away at an early hour in the morning, and she resolved to prepare herself to take that train.

It was a week before her preparations were completed. She had asked her old friend for a small sum of money, and he had not only given her the amount desired, but had insisted upon doubling the sum. Peggy felt conscience-stricken and ungrateful when she took it from his hand; but her face was set and she would not turn back. She had managed during the week to send a box of clothing to the little depot, with word to leave it until called for, and she found herself at last ready to go.

Oh! how inexpressibly sad seemed that last night at home. She hung around Mr. Martin, and his rather unsympathizing, but, after all, good-hearted wife, as if she could not leave them. Once she had got to the door, having bidden them good-night, but she turned at the threshold and, with a sudden impulse, threw her arms around the neck of Mrs. Martin and kissed her, while she burst into a torrent of tears. From her she passed to the old gentleman, who did his utmost to soothe her, until, finally, with a great burst, she flew from the room and shut the door upon them. She did not sleep. All the past, the beautiful, happy past, came back to her. All her petty trials and vexations were as nothing. Every thought, every feeling, save that of gratitude and love for the blessings which that humble couple had showered upon her, was buried innumerable fathoms deep as she ran over her life. She sat down at her writing-desk and literally poured out her heart to them. She begged their forgiveness for the step she was about to take, and which she led them to believe was inspired wholly by her indisposition to endure the coming meeting with Zach. and the obtrusive sympathy of her acquaintances. She promised to keep them informed of her whereabouts, and hoped the time would come when she could return to them and beg their pardon for this seeming ill return for all their kindness. She left the letter on her table blotted with tears, and then, worn out and miserable, she fell asleep in the chair. She roused herself many times during the night, always with a shudder, but never with irresolution, until, finally, she saw the first faint brightening of dawn in the east, and rose to go. She donned her hat and shawl, fell upon her knees once more in the old room where she had spent so many happy hours, and then noiselessly slipped out the rear door, and thence through the stable into the road. The moon was yet shining brightly in the heavens, and cast its gleams like molten silver on the waters of the lake. She was moving on when the sound of voices came from the water, and she turned to listen. It was a song she heard, mellowed and softened by the distance, and came from a party of revelers who were returning from some ball or gathering up the lake. She could hear the dip of the oars keeping time to the measured air, and she sat upon a bank and waited.

"It's so hard," she said, "so hard. I never thought to leave you, dear old hills, and it is not you that have grown hateful to me. No, no. The rocks are always faithful; the trees are green according to promise; the flowers blossom as of old. The very cows in the stable blinked their sleepy eyes lovingly and licked my hand as I passed. All love Peggy save one, and he the one in all whose love she prizes, and he forsakes her." She bowed her head on her breast and the hot tears coursed down her cheeks; still the merry party on the lake drew nearer and the words of their song came more distinctly:

> Spread the white sails to the favoring breeze,
> While over the waters we glide,
> Let the oars dip in the billows so blue,
> Joyfully onward we ride.

Chorus.—

> Hail to the night, hail to the morn,
> Hail to the beautiful sea,
> Dip the oars lightly and merrily sing,
> The bright rippling water for me.

It was a familiar song to Peggy, and it made her task seem harder as she listened:

> Banish all care in this happiest of hours,
> Floating so gladly and free;

Hail to the beautiful waves, silver tipped
By the moon that rides over the sea.

Chorus.—
       Hail to the night, hail to the morn,
       Hail to the beautiful sea,
       Dip the oars lightly and merrily sing,
       The bright rippling water for me.

The party passed, and Peggy rose from her seat and gazed after them.

"Farewell, happy friends," she said. "But for him I might have been one among you to-night, the promised wife, perhaps, of the best, and happiest of you all. It would have been better had he left me in my ignorance, but now I am driven on, an orphan, an outcast — friendless and miserable."

She took one more look at the scene about her, and then turning, as if she feared her resolution might forsake her, dashed almost wildly on her way.

Two hours later she entered a car, among half a hundred drowsy passengers, and with her veil drawn tightly over her face, took a seat in the farthest corner of the close and ill-ventilated

8*   M

coach.   When the conductor approached, shortly
after, she handed him her ticket.   It was long, and
had a number of coupons attached; but the last
bore the name she had so long dreamed about
and pondered over — "Philadelphia."

CHAPTER XII.

MR. BOBBIN LEARNS A NUMBER OF THINGS.

Mr. Timothy Bobbin was fated to two sur-
prises in his experience of Washington life. The
first was the very small figure he cut as an official
of the government, and the second the ease with
which he managed to adapt himself to the duty
required of him. At first he was excessively awkward, and was laughed at somewhat, but there
were too many new-comers in those gray walls to
permit any one person to monopolize the ridicule
of even the few who saw him, and it was not two
weeks before he felt quite at home, and fully equal
to the rather simple tasks assigned him. The
month, however, seemed very long, and Bobbin
had spent his last cent before pay-day came 'round.
When he walked up and received his one hundred
dollars in crisp greenbacks, it seemed to him that

he was on the highway to untold wealth. He
never knew of so much being paid for so little.
The whole thing seemed a sort of joke; and as
he walked down the avenue with this vast sum in
his pocket he wondered how in the world he could
manage to spend it all before the next month
came 'round. Of course a goodly share had to be
sent home, and Bobbin prepared at once to do this.
He felt as if he must send a gift with it, and so he
began looking in the shop windows, endeavoring
to discover something suitable for the occasion.
He found nothing that pleased him until he came
to a jeweler's; but here he stood entranced. After
a while he walked in. At first the prices frightened him, but the high figures, though they dismayed, only made the articles seem more desirable
to the little man. He ended it finally by purchas-
ing a very gaudy, though not strictly pure, necklace, for which he paid twenty-five dollars. This
was for his wife. He then invested in rings for
the children, and his brain fairly throbbed and his
face flushed as he finally departed from the shop

bearing the precious gifts in his hands. What *would* Martin's Corners think when it saw Mrs. Bobbin with that necklace, and the four little Bobbins with those glittering rings on their fingers? He was almost wild when he thought of it. And yet, had the delighted fellow reflected, there was hardly anything in the whole range of purchasable articles that would not have been more appropriate for his purpose. The necklace, which would have done very well for a city girl, full of display and not very particular about quality, was entirely and absurdly out of place on the neck of a thin, pinched, and hungry middle-aged lady in the society of Martin's Corners. Comparatively inexpensive as it was, it so overshadowed and shamed the rest of Mrs. Bobbin's wardrobe that to wear it seemed wonderfully like putting diamond bracelets on a skeleton. And still poor little Bobbin was never so delighted as when he had carefully sealed the packet containing these gifts and deposited it in the express office. He counted the days and hours it would take for the parcel to reach home, and could hardly wait for the time when he would know that his family had received the package and were gloating over the treasures it contained. He had sent fifty dollars in money besides to his wife, and after settling his little bills found himself in possession of nearly twenty dollars as a fund to carry him through the month.

Mr. Bobbin did not see much of Zach. after being installed in his position. Now and then, when he felt particularly in need of a word about home, he went down to Mr. Martin's hotel, and tried to start a conversation, but such visits were not satisfactory. Frequently Zach. was out, at other times occupied, and even when he found him alone there was a sort of air about the new-born statesman that was not encouraging or pleasant. He seemed to Bobbin to be always saying mentally: "Well, this is one of the drawbacks of position — one must receive these persons whether it suits him or not, and be bored, no matter how unpleasant the infliction;" and Bobbin, who with all his simplicity was a sensitive little fellow, could not bear to feel that he was an intruder. He never forgot either how he met Zach. in the park shortly after his arrival, and before he realized the truth of what he now knew, and accosted him as of old, and that Zach. smiled patronizingly and barely touched his hand, turning immediately with a laugh to a couple of fashionable ladies at his side, and saying meaningly, in response to their look of inquiry: "Oh, one of my constituents, such as every member has." He did not intend it for the ear of Bobbin, but the latter heard it, and went away feeling excessively mean and as if he were someway a burden to Zach.

It had been a good while now since Bobbin had even seen his Member. He was getting along well enough with his duties, began to feel quite at home in Washington, and had in a great measure worn off that look of excessive verdancy which he wore when he first came. His clothes, mainly through the little additions which he had made in the way of shirt collars and ties, seemed to have been possibly designed for him. His hat and shoes were brushed, his hair was cut, and he actually wore gloves on Sundays and the more important occasions. His family, too, were looking up at home, but what troubled Bobbin a little was the fact that his wife seemed entering on a sea of extravagance such as he would have deemed impossible. The fact was, that necklace did the business, though Bobbin hardly comprehended it. It had to be worked up to, and necessitated a new wardrobe throughout. And then the house looked shabby by the side of good clothes, and new furniture was ordered. The latter necessity had seemed so imperative that Mrs. Bobbin could not wait for her usual monthly remittance to pay for it, but had it "booked" until that expected arrival. And so it went on, growing worse daily, until in a short time Bobbin could look ahead and see his salary appropriated for a month or two in advance. However, he was not a person to worry, and, except for a word or two of caution to his wife, never complained. Of course she replied that only such things as were absolutely necessary were thought of, and he believed it, wondering all the while how in the world he managed to live before he came into office.

Mr. Bobbin was seated in his modest little room one evening in the early days of April thinking of his coming vacation for a month, at which time he expected to return home, when his landlady entered with a flourish, and informed him that a gentleman wished to speak with him.

"Mr. Martin, he said his name was," exclaimed the woman.

Bobbin started as if he had been shot. The idea of a visit from Zach. had never entered his head. "Why, it's the member from our district," he whispered, and then he rushed past the landlady into the narrow hall. He was hastily hurrying down stairs, when he met Zach. coming up. "I thought I would walk up to your room, Bobbin," said Zach.

Bobbin was of course delighted, but terribly flustrated, and in his excitement caught his toe in a hole in the carpet and fell over on the landing. He got up redder than ever, and encountered his landlady, Mrs. Crispin, standing in the hall where he had left her, rubbing her hands together and bowing.

"Now, Mr. Bobbin," said that lady, "take the parlor; do — it's entirely at your service. I'll keep everybody out; it's too chilly up here."

Bobbin really thought favorably of this plan, for his one room was inconveniently small and rather cold; but Zach. said he could not stay long, and the two passed on. Mrs. Crispin wasn't content, however. She wanted a word more, and she had it.

"You must excuse me, Mr. Martin," said she, smirking dreadfully, "for not a-knowing ye when ye first came in——"

"Oh, certainly," interrupted Zach.

"Mr. Bobbin did not tell me you was coming," she continued. "I s'pose, though, he didn't know it himself."

Here Mrs. Crispin laughed loudly, as if this

fact were immensely funny. Bobbin, who was very mindful of the feelings of anybody and everybody, had paused with his hand on the door to give Mrs. Crispin a chance to get through her speech, and now made a movement to go in, but the lady made another dart forward, saying:

"Next time you come we'll be better fixed, I hope"—and then, without a pause, "Do you know Mr. Jackson, of the House?"

Zach. signified that he had that honor.

"Mr. Jackson used to board with me when I lived on Ninth street," said she. "He's a nice gentleman."

"Oh, yes," replied Zach.

"Give him my respects," said she, "when you see him. He'll remember me. Crispin is the name. Should be glad for you and him to call 'round some evening."

Mrs. C. was going on again, when Zach. made a gesture of impatience, and Bobbin opened his door and let him escape.

Mrs. Crispin was not a bad woman, but she had

that weakness which is almost painful to witness, and yet so common in Washington—the worship of position.   Her judgment of a person was made up from the sort of office he held, and this had become so much a part of her that she never seriously thought of any one as of any consequence whatever who was not in the employ of the government at a good salary.

Bobbin was embarrassed, as we have said, over Zach.'s visit, and he gave him the best chair with a hurried nervousness that revealed the importance which he attached to the call.   Zach., however, did not appear to notice it.   His face was gloomy as he sat down with a sigh.   Bobbin tried to talk on general subjects, but Zach. only looked at him without seeming to understand.   At last he moved restlessly, and said:

"Bobbin, you know Miss Clover, who lives with us?"

"Who, Peggy?" said Bobbin, his face brightening.

"Yes," returned Zach.

"Oh, everybody knows her," said Bobbin.

"Well," continued Zach., hesitatingly, "I don't suppose you are aware of it, but she's left our house."

"Left!" exclaimed Bobbin.

"Yes," said Zach., "gone away in a very strange manner. She wrote a note saying she was going to Philadelphia. Now, what I want to know is, did you ever happen to hear of any friends or relatives she had in Philadelphia?"

"Never," replied Bobbin, "I supposed she was an orphan."

"So she is," returned Zach., "but I thought it barely possible that you had heard of some one she had discovered in that region after I left. The letter that I have got from home don't say anything about that. There is no reason for her going there that I can see, save the fact that she thought to find relatives there."

"It's strange that she should leave your father's," said Bobbin.

Zach. did not answer, but put his hand to his

head, and brought it down slowly over his eyes.

"I think I shall go home pretty soon, Bobbin," said he; "even before the session is over. If you would like to send any word I will let you know before I leave."

Bobbin thanked him. "I hope Peggy will come back," said he, consolingly.

"Yes," responded Zach., "she will, probably. Don't say anything about this matter," he added, "I don't care to have it talked about." And Bobbin promised, though he wondered who he would find in Washington to talk over such a matter as the journeying of a girl from a Western State to Philadelphia. Zach. took his leave soon after, his face bearing the troubled look that it had worn when he entered. The fact was he had been astonished, as well as pained and grieved, to hear of Peggy's mysterious departure. Someway it seemed to show her to him in a new light, and to endear her to him. He was alarmed, however, as well as grieved, and feared that she would fall into bad hands, inexperienced as she was.

It was only a few days subsequent to this that he took the cars for Philadelphia, intending if he heard nothing of her there to go on home. A few days after there appeared in the Philadelphia papers the following advertisement :

PERSONAL—IF PEGGY C., WHO LEFT HOME A few weeks since to come to Philadelphia, will communicate with " Zach.," she will confer a great favor and relieve her friends of much anxiety. Send letter to Continental Hotel for three days.

Zach. waited anxiously, but no reply came. He stayed one day more than he had intended, in hopes of hearing something, but finally despaired of finding her and went on his way. His arrival home was unlooked for, and occasioned surprise. His father received him coldly, and avoided all possible reference to Peggy. Through his mother, however, he learned the full particulars of her going, and was able to judge something of what it had cost her.

"You'd have thought the girl was crazy that

night," said Mrs. Martin. "First a-huggin' me and
then a huggin' the old man, and nearly squeezin'
the breath out o' both of us. The next morning
she was gone, leaving the letter. I never see your
father so worked up. He tore 'round as if he was
wild. He rid a horse barebacked and in a full run
down to the station, but the train had gone, and
Peggy with it. It wuz all I could do to live with
him for a week or so. He wrote, and telegraphed,
and went to see lawyers, and walked the house o'
nights, but finally the letter came from her, and he
quieted down." Zach. held the letter referred to
in his hand, having just read it, and felt much
relieved. It ran thus:

PHILADELPHIA, April 7.

DEAR, DEAR FATHER MARTIN: You must not blame me
nor worry about me. If you only knew what it cost me to
part with you, I know I would not have to ask you twice to
forgive me. I have found a good home here, and the
best and kindest family in the world, after your own. Give
my warmest love to everybody, and write me a good long
letter, addressed to the general Post-office here. I will write
you often, and tell you how I am getting along. Ever your
loving   PEGGY.

"The old man won't trust the letter out of his hands for a minute, scarcely," said Mrs. Martin, "and I had hard work to get it even for you to look at. He seems to be perfectly dazed about that girl, and she was good enough, though I never did see the sense of making so much fuss over her. She was none too polite to me, and used to aggravate me, after you went away, awfully. Only the day afore she got your letter she stuck her head out of the garret winder, as I went into the garden, and sung out:

Hi, Betty Martin, tiptoe, tiptoe,

and in the provokinist way, too, you ever heard. Not that I cared," continued Mrs. M., "only it looked very imperlite for a young lady to be con-ductin' herself like that to one as good as her own mother."

Zach. heard all this and more, and with a grow-ing conviction that he had under-estimated Peggy, and with a return of something of his old love for her which he could scarcely understand. Nothing

makes men or women value one of the opposite
sex, whom they have looked upon as exclusively
their own, so much as the proof that they are
not, after all, indispensable to such person.   A
strange fact, but an indisputable one.   If the
reader doubts it, he may easily convince himself by
a little shrewd practice.

The grave, almost sad, demeanor of Zach. had
its influence on his father, and before many days
the two were friendly again.   It was a sort of satisfaction and atonement to Mr. Martin to see
Zach.'s apparent contrition, and he could not har-
bor resentment toward his only child.   So it came
about that when Zach. finally returned to his
duties, he left home at peace with both his father
and mother, and with a lighter heart.   Another
letter had been received from Peggy, in answer to
that of Mr. Martin, in which, though firmly refusing to return at that time, she promised to come
back some day, "when perfectly cured," and
make her home with them.   She also spoke of
taking a journey with the family in which she had

found a home, a long journey, she said, though without giving the destination; but she assured them that her letters should be as frequent as ever.

And so Zach. went back to Washington. Of course he called on Belle when he returned, and gave her a partial history of the affair at home. He would have told her all, but that young lady turned up her pretty nose and professed to be weary of hearing the wonderful performances of a vulgar country girl constantly narrated, and Zach., with a flush upon his face, not all caused by shame at having dared to recount such a history in her presence, was driven into silence.

But one other circumstance worth relating occurred during the early period of Zach.'s and Bobbin's life in Washington. It was such a revelation to Bobbin, however, that it requires to be mentioned.

One morning Bobbin received a note from Zach., saying that he would address the House that day, and would like to have his constituent present on the occasion. Bobbin was delighted,

being perfectly sure that his friend would electrify
the country, and he at once applied for leave of
absence. This was readily granted, and at an
early hour Bobbin made his way to the Capitol to
make sure of a good seat. It had been announced
that the day would be given up to debate, and the
inexperienced little man believed there would be
some sharp sparring. He was somewhat surprised
upon reaching the House to see both the galleries
and the floor well-nigh deserted, and the least imaginable signs of an intellectual contest. However,
he thought the people had not yet begun to arrive,
and he selected a very eligible seat and prepared
to listen attentively. It was Saturday, a day
known in House parlance as "buncombe day,"
when members who desire to get their speeches
before their constituents, are permitted to repeat
them on the floor, and have them taken down by
the official reporters and printed in the official
"Record;" but Bobbin didn't know anything about
that. He glanced around from time to time,
expecting to behold a rush of visitors; but they

did not come. Away off in a corner of the gentleman's gallery a colored man was fast asleep, and
scattered here and there were four or five other
men, who appeared to fancy the genial warmth of
the chamber. There were no ladies present, the
diplomatic gallery was deserted, and but seven
members were in their seats when Zach. arose to
"address the House." Bobbin was surprised and
hurt. That there should be no more attention
than this shown Zach. was almost like a personal
affront. However, he determined there should be
one attentive listener, and he opened his ears wide
as Zach. began. The speaker's theme was "The
Perils of the Republic," and he dashed into the
subject manfully. Warming up as he progressed,
Zach.'s fine voice rang through the deserted hall,
and Bobbin was amazed that the few persons who
were present did not cheer him. But with the
exception of one other person beside himself,
those present seemed utterly oblivious of Zach.'s
existence. The gentleman in the Speaker's seat
(it was not the Speaker, which Bobbin looked

upon as another insult) was hob-nobbing with a member standing near the chair ; two of the members were writing at their desks, one was lying on a sofa with a handkerchief over his head, and two others were talking to each other, and laughing and slapping their legs near the door of one of the cloak rooms. The one other listener beside Bobbin was a member who sat near and in front of Zach., and who was leaning back in his seat with his feet over a desk, and eating a very red apple. This man watched and listened very closely. At last Zach. paused for a moment, took a swallow of water, and nodded to the man. At this the latter arose and shouted —

"Mr. Speaker!"

"The gentleman from Georgia," said the Chairman.

"I would like to ask the gentleman a question," shouted the stranger, growing very red.

"Does the gentleman consent to be interrupted?" inquired the Speaker.

"Certainly!" responded Zach.

"Of course he does," thought Bobbin. "Just let that fellow with the red head fire away now; Zach. will eat him up if he gets at him."

"I would like to ask the gentleman," pursued the gentleman from Georgia, "whether, in his opinion, the fathers of the Republic ever intended this country to be ruled by thieves and brigands?"

"Certainly not," responded Zach.; "but neither, let me say to my honorable friend, did they intend it to be governed by murderers and banditti."

"Very well!" said the red-headed man, "then why advocate a principle which turns the government over to such men?"

"I beg pardon of my honorable friend," replied Zach., "but I advocate no such principle."

"That red-headed man's a fool," thought Bobbin, "or he never would have dreamt of such a thing."

"But I think different," said the gentleman from Georgia.

"Who cares what you think?" thought Bobbin.

"I am very sorry," replied Zach, "but I am not

responsible for the errors of my honorable friend. He is simply assailing a monster of his own creation."

"That finishes him," thought Bobbin ; and so it did, for the man said no more.

Zach. went on with his speech.   When he came to the peroration the sentences grew very familiar to Bobbin.   He had heard them often in Zach's campaign, and had cheered them to the echo time and again.   He grew enthusiastic once more as he listened, and as Zach. with loud voice and animated gesture appealed to the gallery, his constituent responded as of old, and broke into a clapping of hands and pounding of feet, which made that portion of the building ring.   Immediately the Chairman seized the gavel and began hammering the desk.   This brought Bobbin to a stop.   The few persons in the room were looking at him, most of them with a broad grin on their faces.   The acting Speaker rose very gravely and requested Zach. to suspend his remarks.   Looking toward Bobbin that official said:

"The rules of the House forbid any expressions of approval or disproval from the audience. To violate this rule is a gross discourtesy to this body. If there are any further manifestations of this character the galleries will be cleared, and the Sergeant-at-Arms will see this order enforced."

Then the Speaker sat down and hid his face in his handkerchief. Bobbin felt very small and very guilty after this. He had forgotten all about the rule, even if he had ever heard it, and he didn't know for a while but he had committed a penitentiary offense. However, he sat till Zach. closed his remarks, and then was again amazed to see his idol go off arm in arm with the red-headed member from Georgia who had interrupted him. It could not be that the man had questioned Zach. under a prior agreement, and to make the speech appear natural, and like a genuine debate, in print; and yet it did look suspicious, that's a fact.

When Bobbin met Zach. the latter seemed pleased instead of mortified at the former's applause, and Bobbin himself thought, when he be-

9*

held the speech in the "Record," that it looked
very well to see the sentence, "Loud applause in
the galleries," inserted just at the end of Zach.'s
most brilliant period. Some way it looked as
though the feeling had become so intense that it
had actually burst all bounds, and defied all efforts
at restraint. And so Zach.'s constituents thought
as they read the speech, never dreaming that poor,
humble little Bobbin had alone constituted the
"galleries" that had broken into such an uproar.

CHAPTER XIII.

THREE YEARS AFTER

Three years had elapsed since the incidents recounted in the last chapter. With few exceptions, affairs remained about as they were then. Bobbin's family were in Washington. Barncastle still preyed up and down the avenue, and all the other Washington characters exhibited that unchangeability which seems such a part of society habitues in the Capitol. Zach. had been re-elected, but only after a severe contest in his party convention, and, we are sorry to say, only after pledges of a personal character to rival candidates, which he found it extremely unpleasant to fulfill. Few knew of the caucusing, the consulting, the dickering, the trading, so to speak, that went on before the meeting of the convention which renominated Zach. for the second time. Even Zach. knew com-

paratively little of it. And yet he was largely
responsible. His friends told him what assurances
he ought to give deserving workers, etc., and he
generally yielded to their advice. They assured
him that Snap, who was a dangerous competitor
should he conclude to try his chances, would be
satisfied if he could be reasonably sure of the
Collector's office held by Spiker, and really they
thought that a division was only fair play, and
that Snap should have it. Spiker had held it two
years, and why not give it to Snap?

And Zach., yielding to them, said they could
settle that as they thought fair. And so on. The
result was that Zach. was renominated and re-
elected, Snap working with great zeal for him, and
gaining much credit for his devotion to the "cause"
after the "cause"—i. e., the party—had turned its
back upon him.

When it was determined to remove Spiker and
give the place to Snap, the former should have
been informed of the fact, but this course being
deemed impolitic he was kept entirely in the dark,

and worked like a Trojan for the young man's re-election. It seemed like the deepest ingratitude to remove him, but such a course was demanded, and Zach. wrote a long apologetic and rather gushing letter to Spiker, informing him of the facts, and telling him that he could resign, and thus save appearances.

The rage of Spiker at this knew no bounds. He scorned secrecy. He trumpeted his wrongs to the world. He seemed to want the very rocks to understand the reason of his base betrayal, and he swore eternal vengeance against the men who had brought about his removal, and Zach. Martin in particular. Henceforward there were two wings to the party in that district, and Spiker, loud, bold, and unscrupulous, led the disaffected.

Among those whom the irate ex-Collector called in to help him at this juncture was Bobbin. The latter received a letter recounting the former's wrongs, reminding him of the circumstances of his appointment, and who brought it about, and asking that a close watch be kept on "Mr. Martin's" movements in Washington, and a report made of the same. "You remember your promise," said Spiker, "you stand by me and I'll stand by you. I'm going to beat that muckle-head if it takes every cent I've got in the world."

Bobbin was very much distressed at this. He wanted to serve Spiker, but he could not become a spy in such business. Finally he compromised the matter by writing Spiker that he would do all that he *honorably* could in the way of giving information.

Meantime, strangely enough, Bobbin received a call from Hartwell. Ostensibly Hartwell called on business connected with the insurance company of which he was secretary, but he had a great deal to say about Mr. Martin, and many inquiries to make respecting that gentleman. Among other things he inquired as to the feeling in the district toward Zach., who of his party opposed him there, who had been removed from office, and the name of some of the newspapers of the opposite party. Bobbin freely gave all the information desired, and indeed was rather glad to talk about affairs with which he was so familiar. Hartwell frequently met him after that, and at one time questioned him closely regarding his individual feelings toward Zach., and went so far as to hint at there being a little money in the latter's defeat to one who might assist in compassing it; but this idea was repelled so earnestly, and yet so simply, that Hartwell went no further. Indeed, after that his attentions ceased altogether.

It was only a week or two subsequent that Bobbin received a letter from Spiker upbraiding him strongly, and informing him that he (Spiker) had his eye upon him, and would pay him back. From words used in the letter Bobbin made up his mind that in some way Spiker and Hartwell were corresponding, and both working toward the same end.

Meantime Mr. Barncastle was, as we said, still engaged at his old business. He was the same bland, agreeable gentleman to strangers; the same abiding terror to acquaintances.

It may not be amiss here to introduce the reader to the home of Barncastle — take down the bars, as it were, and drive into his private grounds.

Mr. Barncastle was a boarder; not "permanent," in the special sense in which that term is employed by landladies with yearning rooms to let, for, truth to tell, that gentleman did not, as a rule, tarry long at one place. But now, three years after his introduction to the reader, he was living in the house of a tender-hearted widow named Dabster.

It was a morning in February, and Mrs. Dabster was busily engaged setting Mr. Barncastle's room to rights.

The room contained a bed, a few chairs, a well-worn carpet, a shaky-looking bookcase, a washstand, mirror, and a table with a green cover. On the latter was a model for a monument, made of pasteboard, and looking something like the original design for that exhausted pile at the banks of the Potomac, stunted and woe-begone, which commemorates at the same time the services of

Washington and the disinclination of our people to pay for them. Mrs. Dabster, as we said, was setting the room to rights, and, as she did so, was indulging in a little talk to herself.

"There!" she exclaimed, as she put the finishing touches on her work; "I've done it again. I declare to mercy the pains I take with that man is mor'n many a woman 'ud do for her own husband. And not a 'thank you' do I get for it, to say nothing about money. He hasn't paid me a cent goin' on four months, and seven dollars and twenty-five cents of it borrowed money. But I'll not wait any longer, Mr. Barncastle. Pay you must."

Mrs. Dabster was leaving the room when she heard Mr. Barncastle's voice at the door.

"Come in, Judge!" said he to some one outside. "You won't! Well, then, good-by. Keep the reins taut; mind the fluctuations in the market, and if anything occurs call on me." With this, delivered in the most cheerful tones, Barncastle shut the door and ascended the stairs. When Mrs. Dabster saw him coming she stepped

o

back into the room again and busied herself with the curtains, so that her back was to her boarder when he entered. Mr. Barncastle stopped as he came in, and gazed around with satisfaction.

"There!" he exclaimed, "is what I call a snuggery. There is true comfort and elegance. That is what a female can do. That is what the magical, transforming hand of woman can accomplish. O love! banished from the heart of Barncastle, but still interesting as a scientific curiosity, what wonder that men seek you where alone you can be found in the tender and sympathizing hearts of the daughters of Eve! O! Cupid, cruel, heartless, unrelenting Cupid, do not tempt me. Let me escape!"

Mr. Barncastle stepped into the center of the room, and then appearing to recognize his landlady for the first time, stopped short, striking his favorite attitude.

"Mrs. Dabster," said he, "who would think it of him?"

"Of who?" inquired Mrs. Dabster.

"Of Cupid," responded Barncastle. "So fat, so chubby, so rosy! Pink toes and double chin, and yet what a bare-backed little rascal he is!"

Mrs. Dabster simpered.

"But that aside," continued Barncastle, "let me here and now, Mrs. Dabster, on my knees, figuratively speaking, beg your forgiveness. When I see these attentions which are daily showered upon me, and, above all, when I gaze upon that face unruffled by impatience, undisfigured by avarice, and know at the same moment that beans are sixpence a quart, and veal ribs seven cents a pound, I crimson for my sex."

Barncastle stopped, brushed his handkerchief across his eyes as if to clear away a mist, and straightening up as if determined to immolate himself upon an altar, said solemnly:

"I owe you, Mrs. Dabster thirteen weeks' board ——"

"Fourteen," interrupted Mrs. Dabster.

"Fourteen?" responded Barncastle, as if asking himself a question; "it is, it is, fourteen is the number. Fourteen weeks' board and seven dollars borrowed money."

"And a quarter," put in Mrs. Dabster.

"And a quarter," repeated Barncastle—"so it is again—seven and a quarter. Do I ever forget it? Is it absent from my thoughts by night or by day? The trouble with me, Mrs. Dabster, is that my heart is made of too tender stuff. I wish it was flint, a rock, a mountain of granite," said Barncastle, vehemently.

"Oh, no," said the landlady.

"I do," pursued Barncastle. "Then I should please justice whatever became of mercy. Only yesterday I had that money and was bringing it home to you. I pictured the brightening of the eye, the glad flush of the cheek with which you would receive it, and which it is so charming to behold. On my way I met five orphan children of an old friend. Not a rag to their backs. That is," said Mr. Barncastle, noting a look of incredulity on the Dabster countenance, "not a rag, to speak of. The sight was too much. They had hardly had a glass of water for days. I said to myself, Mrs. Dabster would not hesitate, why should I? Mrs. Dabster would say, 'Have mercy, Barncastle. on the unfortunate,' why should not I say it?

"Mercy," said Mr. Barncastle, striking an atti- tude and quoting Shakespeare from memory—

"Mercy droppeth like the gentle dew from heaven
  Upon the earth beneath. It is twice blessed:
  It blesses him that gives and him that doth receive.

"I gave it. All I had I gave with your bene- diction. Their pretty eyes filled with tears. They cried out: 'Heaven bless you for this act, Mr. Barncastle.' I cried in return: 'Not me, it is not to me, innocent babes, that you are indebted, but to that tender-hearted and absolutely unmatchable woman, Mrs. Dabster.'"

Mrs. D. was quite affected by this time, and begun wiping her eyes with the corner of her apron.

"Do not weep," said Barncastle, soothingly; "they are happy now. They are blessed in receiving; you in giving. But alas, my friend, where am I?" Here Barncastle heaved a prodigious sigh, and with a look of despair began walking the floor. "Yes," said he, halting in front of ·her; "if it is not asking too much of your patience, I ask, where am I?"

"Why," said good Mrs. Dabster, innocently, "you are here where you ought to be."

Barncastle took another turn or two across the room, and then halting again, said earnestly: "Mrs. Dabster, why are men born, as it were, in indigent circumstances? Why are we created to endure the pangs of poverty, the pains of unrequited affection, the embarrassments of undischarged obligations, the agony of disordered livers, when we might be playing leap-frog, so to speak, in infinite space, the unfledged denizens of a sphere where nobody is poor? Why am I not a germ," said Barncastle, clasping his hands and gazing longingly at the ceiling, "a germ nestling in the bosom of the universe, instead of an unfortunate fellow being of yours (here his eyes rested

on the form of Mrs. Dabster) in want of a beg-
garly five dollar note? Five dollars," said he,
snapping his fingers contemptuously. "Five dollars! I shall have a remittance to-morrow; but
for the want of a little five dollars to-day I lose a
hundred. Think of that, and then talk of misery!
If I were not immersed, as it were, in a whirlpool
of debt to you, I would ask the loan of a V until
a quarter before six to-morrow evening."

Barncastle watched the effect of this announcement on Mrs. Dabster, and was evidently encour-
aged to proceed.

"There!" he exclaimed, "crushing my pride,
trampling my sensitiveness under my feet, I do
ask it — I do, Mrs. Dabster."

The lady looked at him for a moment with a
sort of anxious, puzzled expression before she
replied. Barncastle stood like another Essex,
proudly awaiting his doom.

"You'd be certain to pay it back to-morrow?"
she said, doubtingly.

"Certain!" repeated Barncastle, looking hurt

at the faintest doubt of the possibility of his failure. "Madam! you do not know me. Absolutely
certain, Mrs. Dabster, absolutely."

"Because," said that lady, apologetically, "one
as tries to feed government clerks and fresh members at six dollars a week, including lunches, has
all she can possibly do to keep along, Mr. Barncastle."

"Alas, I know it," he replied. "There's the one
item of molasses. As I have watched the miracu-
lous disappearance of that saccharine article, my
heart has overflowed with sympathy for you. I
have wondered how you endured it. I have asked
myself where in the wide world all this molasses
came from. Where it goes to is plain enough. If
there is one weakness worthy of study, one that
merits scientific examination, it is the weakness
among government clerks for molasses."

"There!" said Mrs. Dabster, handing him the
money. "I hope you will not fail, Mr. Barncastle,
knowing my circumstances."

"Fail!" exclaimed Barncastle, deftly transferring the note to his vest pocket; "if you were as sure of a husband, such as you deserve, as you are of this five dollars——"

"O, *Mr.* Barncastle," interrupted the lady, trying to look indignant, "how dare you?"

"Ah!" continued her boarder, noting her weak spot and chucking her under the chin. "There are days of bright connubial bliss before you yet, Mrs. Dabster. Hoping they may come speedily and remain forever, there!"—and amazing as it may seem, Barncastle absolutely kissed the widow. Mrs. Dabster blushed and uttered the regulation scream, and was about to scold her boarder for taking such liberties, when the door-bell rang, and she glided down stairs. In a moment she returned, and informing Mr. Barncastle that a gentleman wished to see him, ushered into his presence Richard Hartwell.

10

CHAPTER XIV.

IN WHICH PEGGY APPEARS IN A NEW ROLE.

We leave Barncastle and his caller for a short time to look elsewhere.

Seven days out from her European port of departure, a Cunard steamship was plowing swiftly through the Atlantic, her prow turned toward the New World. It was a half hour after sunset, and a hundred passengers were gathered on deck enjoying the fresh air and the beautiful scene. At one side sat a party of three, one a tall, dark, elderly lady, stately and dignified, and yet with a wonderfully kind expression in her face. Another, a young man very stylish and handsome, and a third a young lady, lithe and graceful, and with dark eyes that danced with merriment now and then, but bore oftener a far-away look that seemed to wander from the beautiful evening scene to others, perhaps less pleasant though more fascinating.

"I wonder how far your thoughts have traveled in the last five minutes, Miss Cristopher," said the young man, after waiting all that time to hear the young lady speak.

Miss Cristopher called back her wandering gaze, and smiled half-reproachfully as she answered:

"Now, it really has not been five minutes, Mr. Bruce."

"Nearer ten," he answered. "I appeal to Madame Benedict if it has not."

The stately lady smiled and confirmed the young man.

"Well, I am very sorry," said Miss Cristopher, "but the evening seems designed for reflection."

"But not sad reflection," responded the young gentleman. "Come, now, it is desecration to look sad on such a night."

"I hope I was not really looking disconsolate," said the young lady.

"Indeed you were, absolutely weary of life. Come, now, confess where your thoughts were running. Was it back to the old land or forward to the new?"

"Forward," said she, "that much I will tell you. The despair which you saw came from the Republic, which is just ahead, and not from the Kingdom which we have left behind," and she laughed pleasantly.

"But it ought to be a happy and expectant look," continued Mr. Bruce, the name of the young gentleman. "You, above all others, ought to be jubilant,.and yet you are moping dreadfully."

"Now, shame," said Miss Cristopher; "you know I have been excessively animated ever since we left Liverpool. If you do not stop slandering me in such a way I shall conceal myself like the veiled prophet, and you shall see only my hand. That won't look mournful, I am sure."

"It will," replied the young man, "it does already. It seems to be tinged by your eyes, and looks as sad as your face. You must wear gloves when you disguise yourself, or I shall detect your despair just as easily as now."

The banter, which was largely in earnest, went on for some time, until finally the two ladies went below.

"Margaret," said the elder, addressing the girl, "what are you going to do with Mr. Bruce?"

The young lady threw her arms about the neck of Mrs. Benedict, and said, softly, "I do not know."

"He will declare himself," said the lady, " unless you restrain him."

"I think so," said Margaret. " Indeed, I fear so."

" He is a young man of excellent family," continued Mrs. Benedict, "wealthy, educated, irreproachable."

"Yes," answered Margaret.

"What will you do then, my dear?" said the former, supporting the head of the young lady and smoothing her brown hair tenderly.

"I do not wish to marry," said Margaret.

"Then you will refuse him?" said her companion. "My dear, have you ever reflected that you are declining a great many brilliant offers?"

"Yes," said Margaret, demurely; "I have thought of it."

"And resolved to do no better?" pursued Mrs. Benedict, smiling, half-reproachfully.

"What can I do?" said the girl, appealingly. "You with your good heart and wise head, tell me."

"You do not love Mr. Bruce?" inquired Mrs. Benedict.

"Oh, no!" said Margaret.

"Not even a little?"

"I should say not a particle," replied the young lady, frankly.

"He is a man that most women would greatly admire," said her companion.

"Oh, yes," responded Miss Cristopher, "and I admire him and respect him."

"But can not love him?"

"No."

"That old affection clings to you yet, driving

out all others; I see, I see," said Mrs. Benedict, sadly.

"No, not that," replied the girl; "all that is dead, but, someway, nothing comes in its place."

"Well, well, my dear," said Mrs. Benedict, smiling; "you must do the best you can, and, above all, you must save Mr. Bruce the pain of a refusal. Do that in some manner; your own heart and good sense will tell you how." And here the conversation terminated.

The next evening Miss Cristopher and Mr. Bruce were slowly walking back and forth on deck. Now and then they stopped to gaze down into the waves that dashed their phosphorescent light against the plunging prow of the vessel, and again at the starlit heavens that sparkled above them.

"To-morrow," said the young man, "one day more and this trip will come to an end."

"And we shall be there," said Miss Cristopher, beckoning with her head toward the great Continent. "At home once more. O! how nervous I get over it."

"And you are glad," said he. "You do not feel a pang at terminating the voyage? I had hoped you would."

"Oh, you mistake me there," responded Miss Cristopher, ashamed of her thoughtlessness. "Of course I shall deeply regret parting from all our friends on the ship."

"And may I hope that I do not occupy the least place among them?" said he.

"Oh, you know you are the very first," said Miss Cristopher, frankly. "We never could have done at all without you."

She was sorry a moment after that she had been so outspoken, for the young man grew very serious, and finally, taking her hand, began the long-feared declaration. The young lady was frightened, and blamed herself for it all; but she resolved to stop him at every hazard. He had barely got the preliminary sentence out of his mouth before she deliberately put both her hands

over that organ of speech, and threatened to stifle
him if he said another word. It was a novel way
of preventing an offer, but it was very effective.

"Now stop," said she; "you mustn't, and that's
the end of it."

"I won't," said he, with a voice that sounded
very much muffled as it came from behind the
palm that had been placed upon his mouth. "I
won't, if you will keep your hands just where they
are for ever."

"But, really, now," pursued the young lady,
"you must say no more upon that subject."

"How do you know what I was going to say?"
said he.

"Well, I have a premonition," she answered.

"You are used to it," he said.

"Shame upon you for that," returned Miss Cristopher.

"Well, then, you are engaged," said the young
man.

"Please, now, do not allude to it any further,"
she replied.

10*   P

"I will not, except this," he said. "If you are not engaged, you shall say no. If you are, remain silent. Come, now that's only fair. So I ask the question, 'Are you engaged?'"

Miss Cristopher saw no better way of escaping, so she adopted this plan and said nothing. Mr. Bruce thereupon congratulated her, though sadly, and only asked that they might continue to meet as friends. Then there were good-nights, and the young lady went below. Once there she fell to telling her stately companion of the interview, and while they regretted the occurrence and sympathized with the disappointed lover, they could not resist laughing over the odd means employed by the young lady to prevent a declaration.

It was ten o'clock the next morning when the great ship with her decks swarming with the aroused passengers slowly made her way through the innumerable water craft up to the great docks. The latter were thronged with expectant faces, eagerly turned upward to the crowded decks of

the incoming ship. Close by the railing stood
Mrs. Benedict, Miss Cristopher, and Mr. Bruce.
The young lady's eyes were anxiously turned on
the faces looking up to her. All at once she gave
a glad start, and waved her hand and handkerchief
at some one on the docks, while the tears sprung
to her eyes. At the same moment a hat went up
from the crowd, and the person that she had recognized seemed trying to clamber over everybody
else and make his way toward the gangway. Certainly at a distance the enthusiastic individual
looked strangely like old Mr. Martin, and—well—
could it be possible—was the young lady on the
great ship, with her mouth all smiles and her eyes
all tears, actually Peggy!

CHAPTER XV.

PLOTS.

"Mr. Barncastle, I believe," said Hartwell, advancing.

Barncastle did not know the young man before him, but it occurred to him at once that it must be some one of his numerous creditors. He knew of no one else who would be likely to have business with him, and he answered accordingly.

"Yes, certainly; by the way this is a most unfortunate thing, Mr.——, Mr.——"

"Hartwell," interrupted the young man, presenting a card.

"Hartwell," repeated Barncastle. "As I was saying, this is most unfortunate. Do you know that not an hour ago I was chasing for you up and down, in and out the hotels, through the restaurants and clubs, with the money in my hand to pay

you. High nor low—nowhere could I find you,
and now, not five minutes ago, I lent the money,
every cent, to my good landlady who is in great
trouble—lost a son—blowed up on the railroad
—all that sort of thing—horrible affair—so you
see I'm down, so to speak—flat."

While Barncastle had been speaking, Mr. Hartwell had been looking at him puzzled and bewildered, not knowing what he was driving at.

"Come," said Barncastle, noting what he thought
a disappointed expression—"don't let it trouble
you. It's a sure thing, you know. Just name the
spot you will be in at eighteen minutes to three
to-morrow afternoon, and all you will have to do is
to reach out your hand and take the money. Let
me see, what is the amount?"

Hartwell, who began to see the point, now
interrupted. "You mistake, Mr. Barncastle," said
he. "You certainly do not owe me anything."

"What!" exclaimed Barncastle, "is it possible
that in this dim light I have been misled by the
facial expression and the similarity of names?

Why, so I have. My dear sir, let me apologize,"
and Barncastle seized the hand of Hartwell and
wrung it with great fervor. "I took you," he continued, "for a member, an old friend to whom I
promised a subscription for the orphan asylum. A
thousand pardons."

"Do not make any apologies," said Hartwell.
"I came here on a little business, and may as well
get at it at once. I know something of your influence with members of Congress, Mr. Barncastle,
and that, frankly, is why I came."

Barncastle was flattered, as Hartwell intended
he should be.

"My dear sir," said Barncastle, "I never boast
of these things. They are matters that require
reticence and diplomacy."

"Multiplication, division, and silence, eh," said
Hartwell.

"My *dear* sir, you have spoken it," responded
Barncastle.

"You seem to be very comfortable here," said
Hartwell, looking around the room.

"Neat, neat," replied Barncastle ; "but by no means extravagant. I scorn pomp, Mr. Hartwell. My library, not large but select, is all the luxury that I indulge in ; but without books, without these companions of my quiet hours, life would be dreary indeed."

It was well that Mr. Barncastle's book-case was closed, otherwise he would never have ventured to speak so grandly of his library. The fact was that the ancient case, rickety and dingy, contained at that moment a shaving-mug, a box of pills, three or four half-empty bottles of patent medicines, and a variety of old traps, but not even the faintest sign of a book of any description. His enthusiasm on the subject of his library was therefore purely fictitious.

Hartwell glanced at the book-case as if he could see through the doors the treasures within, and then turned to the table.

"What have you here? he said, pointing to Barncastle's model for a monument.

The latter threw himself back with an air of

pride as he answered. "Ah," said he, "there you touch me, Mr. Hartwell. Now you hit upon my weakness. That," said Mr. Barncastle, taking the model by the top and turning it round, "is the fruit of—well, you may call it eccentricity, if you will. Who knows a man so well as himself; who knows the secrets of his heart, the purity of his intentions, the loftiness of his aspirations, as he knows them? You answer, nobody! So say I. If, then, a man be honest, none can tell so well as he what he deserves of his country. I feel here, for instance, a heart throbbing with compassion. I have here a brain bursting with patriotic fire. I have here a form ready to be sacrificed on the altar of liberty. What, then, do I do? I design with the utmost impartiality a monument for posterity. It will be a flat shaft, one hundred feet in height. On one side will be a phœnix rising from its ashes, typical of what may be expected of Ebenezer Barncastle. On the reverse, the inscription you see here in German text:

TO THE MEMORY OF

EBENEZER BARNCASTLE, F. R. S.,

A POLITICAL PHILOSOPHER,

WHOSE EXTENSIVE KNOWLEDGE OF CURRENT EVENTS WAS ONLY
EQUALED BY HIS SURPASSING FACULTY OF
MASSING FACTS AND FIGURES

FOR THE

BENEFIT OF HIS COUNTRYMEN.

AN ADEPT AT THE TARIFF, AT HOME ON THE FINANCES,
HE LIVED TO ADORN THE EIGHTEENTH CENTURY,

AND DIED REGRETTED BY A MOURNING WORLD.

HIS MOTTO HE TRANSMITS TO HIS DESCENDANTS,
" ORGANIZE."

For a while Mr. Hartwell stared at this epi-
taph, lost in amazement. The curious thing
about the matter was the utter seriousness with
which Barncastle regarded it. He did not seem to
see the least impropriety in the idea, but to look
upon it as a great discovery he had wrought and
was soon to bestow upon a suffering world, no
matter how ungrateful that world might be. It
was some time before Hartwell could overcome his
astonishment and enter upon the real object of his
visit. Finally he composed himself, and began :

"You know the Hon. Zachariah Martin?" he said, at length.

"Know him!" responded Barncastle; "intimately. Indebted to me for his position, for the clothes on his back, for the money in his pocket; borrows of me—this is confidential, of course?"

"Certainly."

"Borrows of me largely. Too largely, I fear; still, Zach. is a very clever young man, and I can not be hard upon him."

"Then you are the very man I have been looking for," responded Hartwell. "To come right down to business, we want to get a favor of Martin."

"I see."

"We want him to do us a favor, and we are ready to pay for it."

"Exactly."

"In this package," pursued Hartwell, taking out a large envelope, "is a letter addressed to him by a friend of his, a lady, asking the favor alluded to. In this other package are five thousand dollars of bonds in the Nantucket Insurance Company. We propose to give him these bonds for doing our work; but of course this is not to be intimated by the person presenting the package."

"Of course not," echoed Barncastle.

"We want him to get these bonds through one who can testify to the fact should Mr. Martin desire, for any reason, to play us falsely hereafter. Now, Mr. Barncastle, we have thought you the man to hand them to him. For doing this, a very great favor to us, we will pay you one hundred dollars now and one hundred dollars more when you testify to that fact, if such time ever arrives. You can say that the package was sent to him by the lady who sent the note, with a request that he retain them for her. The rest he will understand. Now, Mr. Barncastle, what do you say?"

"My dear sir," responded the latter, "consider it done—for a friend. He can refuse me nothing. He's too deep in, you see, too deep in," and Barncastle put his finger to his nose significantly.

"I see," said Hartwell.

"Money is nothing to me" continued Barn-castle. "Consider it done, as I said before, for a friend."

Hartwell was puzzled at this. He had esti-mated Barncastle pretty fairly, and besides he had heard enough of him to know that he was a very impecunious old vagabond, and yet here he was declining money for his services. Without attempting to fathom the mystery, and glad to save the one hundred dollars if he could accom-plish his object as well, he rose to go. He shook Barncastle warmly by the hand. He had reached the door and was about turning the knob when a thought seemed to strike the latter.

"One moment," said Mr. Barncastle; "I am not ordinarily in this business. My sphere is gen-erally broader and my terms higher. Money, as I said before, is no object to me but—as a—a guaranty—of—good faith, you know, hey?" And Barncastle smiled his blandest. Hartwell smiled also, showing his white teeth, but his smile was not so genial as that of Barncastle.

"Oh, of course," said he. "I shall gladly pay you. I only thought —"

"Not that," said Barncastle, moving the palm of his hand deprecatingly. "It is not the money, you know, but — but the — indefinable — pledge of sincerity, you know — between — ah — gentlemen, as it were. Hay, right?"

"Exactly," said Hartwell, and without further ado he placed one hundred dollars in Mr. Barncastle's extended hand.

"I will call to hear the result," said he, and once more moved toward the door. With many a wave of the hand Barncastle bowed his visitor out, not satisfied until the outer door had closed upon him. Then he returned to his room, with an expression of wonderful exultation on his face.

He held the money and the bonds in his hand and gazed at them. "What's their game?" said he, musingly. "A letter, too; a mysterious letter. I ought to know, as the confidential agent of these parties, what said letter contains. I will know. It's unprofessional, but prudent," and with that Barn-

castle broke the seal and read the following
note:

DEAR MR. MARTIN: I want the young man of whom I
spoke appointed sure — to some good place in the revenue
service. You said any thing in your keeping was at my disposal. All I have to offer in return I give. Is the consideration sufficient? Reply by the bearer.   Your loving
                                                        BELLE.

Barncastle folded the letter thoughtfully.

" His loving Belle," he echoed. "This ought
to be sufficient without the bonds. I wonder if it
wouldn't be. Five thousand dollars!" Barncastle
was gazing thoughtfully at the papers when there
was a knock at the door. "Come in," said he,
turning his face to the entrance and putting his
bonds behind him. At his summons Mrs. Dabster
entered. Barncastle looked at her majestically.
"Come here," he exclaimed, and Mrs. Dabster
approached.

"I owe you divers sums," said he, loftily; "I
know nothing about the total. How much is it?"

Mrs. Dabster was astonished, but she quickly
gave him the amount.

'Here's ten dollars," said Barncastle, handing her a bill. "Of the balance we will speak at another time."

" Now, look here," he continued, and he opened the rich-looking bonds and exhibited them to her astounded vision, holding them at a safe distance.

"Oh!" exclaimed Mrs. Dabster, "what are they?"

"Governments," said Barncastle. "Government bonds bearing six per cent. in gold, payable semi-annually. Every dollar of 'em worth a dollar and twenty cents."

"My gracious!" returned Mrs. Dabster. "How many of them are there?"

"Thousands, millions perhaps," said Barncastle. "Don't touch them. Ah ha! it scorches your boarding-house eyelids to look at 'em, don't it?"

"Please don't speak to me that way," pleaded the landlady.

"Speak that way? I'll speak any way. I owe you money, *you*," said Barncastle. "Why then take it and leave me! Ha, ha, begone, woman!"

"Oh, I would rather you would never pay me than to talk so to me," said she, whimpering.

"Talk," said he. "Here, by the soul of Napoleon, I'll act as well as talk. What's your wheezy furniture worth; make out your bill and consider it smashed."

"Don't," begged Mrs. Dabster, as Barncastle tipped over a chair. "Don't please, kind, good Mr. Barncastle. Oh, dear, I believe you've gone mad. I'm going to faint, I am — I am —"

"Well, faint," said he, "and thank your stars that you can fall into the arms of a Barncastle."

Mrs. Dabster would have carried her threat into execution, but suddenly a thought seemed to strike her boarder, and jamming his hat on his head he rushed out into the street.

CHAPTER XVI.

IN WHICH CLOUDS APPEAR ON ZACHARIAH MARTIN'S HORIZON.

It was quite early in the Spring, and Congress was still in session, when there appeared in the Hiltonville " Banner " the following notice.

INDIGNATION MEETING!

CITIZENS, ATTEND.

All citizens, without regard to party, are requested to meet at the Court House this evening to express their indignation at the course of our Representative in Congress. Those who wish to frown down the notorious attempt of our member to peddle official patronage and sell the people's offices to the highest bidder are earnestly requested to attend.

This notice was unsigned, but it originated with Spiker, who was actuated quite as much by per-

sonal spite, it may well be supposed, as by anxiety
for the purity of the public morals. During the day
a number of gentlemen who had reasons more or
less important for giving Zach. a blow were busy
drumming up an audience. It was queer under
what curious and diverse influences they worked.
Of course Spiker wanted revenge. So did five
candidates for postmaster, whose claims had been
disregarded in favor of the sixth appointee. So
did several unsuccessful applicants for other places
who were sure they failed to receive certain offices
in Zach.'s gift because he was either an idiot, a
corruptionist, or was unmindful of his duty. The
ranks of these were augmented by a dozen people
who personally disliked the young man. One
thought him proud. Another many years previ-
ously had had a disagreement with his father.
Another had always said he was not the right man
for Congress, and still another was jealous of
Zach., and always had been, and was ready to fly
at anything as an excuse for denouncing him.

A man had better be a digger and delver

among men than to struggle an inch only above those who have always known him. He must reach an ell, rise clear and unmistakably above them, or his life is that of a slave and a martyr combined.

Of course joined to all these we have named were the political enemies of Martin, the "men on the other side," who always esteem it the first duty they owe the country to cry down every one and everything having any connection with the opposing party. These came out with a relish. Then there was a class of staid citizens who rarely took much part in active politics, whose presence it was deemed necessary to secure. This was done to a degree through personal solicitation, by appeals to them to turn their faces against alleged corruption, and by that flattery which old stagers know so well how to use when occasion requires. The result was that there was really a formidable gathering, representing to a great extent the best element of Hiltonville and the surrounding country. By what seemed a spontaneous movement one of the oldest and most respectable merchants of the town was chosen to preside. The truth was that he had been visited the day before and urged to attend, being informed that he would be chosen. He was flattered to be deemed the one man most fit to grace the seat of the president of such a gathering, and finally consented. When, therefore, a voice in the audience called the assemblage to order, and nominated Madison Goldstone for chairman, a loud aye went up from the meeting, which really seemed astonished when that gentleman came promptly forward and took the chair.

Mr. Goldstone, prior to being waited upon as aforesaid, had heard little and cared less about Zach.'s alleged shortcomings; but suddenly he was filled with the deepest concern for the country and the honor of her public servants. This was commendable, but abrupt. However, he made an excellent speech, pointing out the absolute necessity of integrity and exalted virtue in public life, and sat down amid loud applause. Another

prominent citizen, who had been spoken to in like
manner, was called upon, and made a similar
speech. Seeing such men, persons unaccustomed
to "meddling with politics," active and interested,
the lesser lights sprang up, and the meeting really
waxed indignant. One gentleman explained the
nature of the charges against Zach., and the proof.
The principal one was that he had secured the
appointment of a non-resident of the district in a
manner that smacked strongly of bribery. A
committee on resolutions was appointed, and retired to an ante-room. Here the chairman, who
had been selected days beforehand, and had been
furnished with a set of resolutions ready made
from the hands of the editor of the Hiltonville
" Banner," drew those resolutions from his pocket
and submitted them to the committee. One active member moved to strike out "a" in the second
line of the fourth resolution and substitute "the,"
which motion was carried. Another suggested
that "reported" charges would be better than
"alleged" charges, but after considerable debate

the sentence was allowed to remain as it was. After much discussion, but no more changes, the committee returned, looking like a jury in whose hands hung life or death, and marched solemnly into the assemblage. Their appearance was greeted with applause. Each resolution, as it was read, was greeted with more applause, and the full set was adopted with a loud aye. It is needless to recount them. They were like the resolutions of every other like meeting, very long, very heavy, and very unjust. But the object was accomplished. The next issue of the "Banner" had a full account of the gathering, with the proceedings and resolutions in full. It gave the names of the officers, speakers, and prominent persons present, and singularly enough scarcely one of the real instigators and manipulators of the affair was mentioned. The meeting appeared to be a spontaneous assemblage of indignant citizens who, scandalized and outraged, had at last aroused from their lethargy and asserted their rights. It was a great success.

Zach. had been warned of these impending

troubles. He had been told that if he expected
to secure a renomination he must send explana-
tions of his conduct, and must prepare himself for
a furious fight. But to all these warnings he
turned a deaf ear. To explain the appointment
which he had made at the request of Belle, would
be embarrassing. To pursue and fight down every
other slander that was put in circulation against
him required too much time and patience, and he
resolved to let matters take their course. "I have
lived among these people for nearly thirty years,"
he wrote. "If, without proof, they can believe me
guilty of such crimes as they charge upon me, I
shall not attempt to undeceive them. It simply
shows for how little an honest life counts, after all."

* * * * *. * * *

Bobbin never would have believed it cost so
much to live in Washington. His family were
with him now, and he occupied a very pleasant
little house on " O " street, " Northwest." The old
neighbors of Mrs. Bobbin would never have recognized in the rather trim and neat appearing mis-

tress of that little house their old acquaintance at Martin's Corners. The playmates of the younger Bobbins would have been overwhelmed by the appearance of these youthful aristocrats now, in their starched pinafores and their top boots. It was Mrs. Bobbin's darling dream to put Johnnie into a blue suit with dazzling brass buttons, set off by a cap with gold lace around the brim; but do what she would, and "skimp" as much as she might, she could never reach the fruition of that lofty hope. The fact of it was Bobbin's purse was always empty long before pay-day, and his debts were still accumulating. Every month left a little larger balance at the butcher's and the grocer's, and he saw only one hope of getting even, to wit: promotion—that dream of the government clerk. When Mrs. Bobbin came on with the family she brought with her five hundred dollars, the proceeds of the sale of her little home at Martin's Corners. She felt almost a million-aire, and seriously thought of buying a home in Washington suited to her advanced condition in life. But when she arrived in that city she found she could hardly do this. The little bit of furniture she brought with her seemed very shabby and out of place in her new house, and before she had the rooms arranged to her fancy she had expended her five hundred dollars and had a pretty little balance still to pay at the furniture store. And so, though the good woman would never have believed it possible that she could be anything but content in such a house and with such surroundings, she really found herself very unhappy and very envious, and very impatient with poor little Bobbin, who, in spite of all, maintained his cheerfulness, and was immensely pleased and comparatively happy.

Mrs. Bobbin kept a servant, too. Gracious! how the people at home would have stared at that. This servant was nothing to speak of; that is, she was very little and very cheap; but then she had a prodigious appetite, and as provisions were dear the Bobbins found her a rather expensive luxury. But Mrs. Bobbin got the most out

11*

of her — not so much in work as in appearance.
If anybody called, that lady would under no circumstances consent that any of the family should
go to the door. Angelica — for this was the small
servant's name — was called upon for such duty.
She was not exactly adapted to this service, for
she always presented a sort of wet appearance, as
if she had just been washed but not wiped, and as
she opened the door she would invariably look
straight past the visitor at the crowds of children
gamboling in the streets. When the sight was
particularly animating, Angelica would give a
bound or two on her own account, much like a
high-fed carriage horse excited by the antics of a
drove of colts in a neighboring field. After
prancing awhile in this manner, she could be
brought by degrees to comprehend the questions
of the caller, and after a time generally managed
to answer them. To Bobbin, Angelica was one of
the enigmas of the universe. Whenever she was
present he seemed lost in the contemplation of
her. She had a queer way of always addressing

her master as *Mes*ter, with a spiteful explosion on the first syllable that sounded a good deal like pulling the cork out of a bottle of pop. At first the little man did not like this. It startled him, and some way made him feel as though he was being called into court by a bailiff. But gradually he became reconciled.

"She's an orphan, poor thing," said he, "and if she gets a minute's happiness from firing my name off in that style, why let her do it. Though, to tell the truth," he added in an undertone to one of the children, "it *is* unpleasant, that's a fact."

. CHAPTER XVII.

BARNCASTLE AGAIN.

It was the last month of Spring, and Zach. was waiting to know the result of the convention in his district which was to nominate a candidate for his place. He was pretty confident that his friends would carry him through, but he was anxious and uncomfortable. It was arranged that his marriage with Belle should take place in July, though no public announcement had been made of the fact. Through his father, Zach. had heard three or four times from Peggy, but only to the effect that she was getting along comfortably. All his efforts to learn her whereabouts failed, for if his father knew he would not tell. Many a time Zach., wearied with care and disappointment, felt as if he would fly to Peggy if he only knew where she was, and give up all — even Belle — for a little of the old-time peace and affection. But this was not to be, and when his low spirits would depart, and he would see Belle, radiant and beautiful, admired and courted, he turned to her, for the time being, content again.

It was a very bright morning in the latter part of May, and Zach. was seated in his room at the Arlington looking over his newspaper mail. He opened the Hiltonville "Banner," and in great, black head-lines on the first page saw the following:

OUR MISREPRESENTATIVE.

———

A CHEAT AND A SNEAK.—HE IS AFTER SPOILS.

———

The Janus-faced upstart who misrepresents this district in Congress is again called upon to explain. Let him answer if he dare the following plain inquiries:

Who voted millions of the people's money away in that stupendous swindle, the deepening of Duck Creek.

Who put through the outrageous private land swindle of Peter McDoosen, by which $300,000 of the public funds were worse than squandered?

Who was BRIBED to secure the appointment of an entire stranger and non-resident in the revenue service of this district?

Who was drunk on last Thanksgiving-day in Washington, and was carried home in a scavenger's cart by the police?

Let the sovereign people rise and demand an answer

Zach. read all this and much more with a flushed and angry face. "And. this," he said to himself, "is the reward of patient and honest labor. Will the people credit such slanders? Can they be so unjust to one who has served them faithfully? Ah, well, we shall see."

He put down the "Banner" and took up a Washington newspaper. He glanced carelessly over the columns until his eye finally lighted upon the following paragraph :

The great portrait of the late President, by Miss Margaret Cristopher, which the government has purchased at a high figure, and which has been so warmly praised by European critics, will be exhibited to a few invited guests at the Arlington House parlors, this evening at 8 o'clock. There is much curiosity manifested so see a lady who has suddenly dawned on the world of art like a meteor, and when we say she is young and beautiful, as well as rich and famous, this interest will certainly not be decreased.

"Humph!" said Zach. "I remember that I

promised Belle to attend. They are certainly making a great deal of ado over this artist."

Zach. fell to reflecting again, when he was roused by a knock. In response to his summons to enter, the door opened and Mr. Ebenezer Barncastle appeared. Zach. looked up but turned away with impatience, and taking up a newspaper buried himself in the telegraphic dispatches. Mr. Barncastle entered, removed his hat with the grace of a Chesterfield, and, looking about him with a smile, proceeded to pull off his brown cotton gloves.

" Mr. Martin," said he gaily, looking about the room, " Here you are, cradled, as it were, in the lap of luxury. Fine hotel, elegant appointments, matchless *cuisine*. Humph, gad! what do they charge you here by the month? Lucky dog, lucky dog. There's nothing like genius, especially when united to wealth. Martin," continued Barncastle, taking a seat with great freedom, "I am very glad to see you. I want to have a confidential talk with you. Do you know," here Barncastle drew his seat nearer and spoke slowly and impressively, "it's my opinion that the country is going straight to the devil in a coach and six. Hey?"

Zach. still remained buried in his newspaper, and Barncastle went on:

"You do not answer," said he. "Ah, well, public men do not like to express opinions, but they feel for the country as we feel for it; their hearts are wrung, as ours are wrung; they see the danger as we see it. *Mister* Martin"—here Barncastle grew earnest and vehement—"how shall the honest men of this country save the republic?"

Barncastle dropped his chin deep down in his shirt-collar and looked out from under his eyebrows at Zach. as he asked this question.

"How shall they save it? There is but one way, organize! bring out the voters! watch the polls! Let every man devote one day to the service of his country. Organize the wards, the townships, the counties. Rouse the people to action. Appoint committees, form clubs; bring in the sick, the halt, the lame, the blind, the indigent; spur up the indifferent, labor with the hesitating, cleave to the irresolute, stiffen up the backbone of the workers, and give the men of sediment a chance at glory. By action, ceaseless united action, this fabric of ours may yet be preserved. You understand me, hey? Right!"

Zach. was growing intensely disgusted.

"Barncastle," said he, finally, "I wish you wouldn't bother me."

"What!" exclaimed that patriot, drawing back with astonishment. "Are you, too, lukewarm in the cause?"

"Oh, you are such a prodigious fraud!" said Zach., gazing wearily at him.

Barncastle drew back again with offended dignity.

"Mr. Martin," said he, "I *am* your debtor. I am, sir; I admit it. I have had the sum about me a dozen times within the past twenty-four hours, but, unfortunately, at such times I was unable to discover you. It's annoying, but it's

R

perfectly true, and might happen to any one.
Now, when I have parted with the money, I
stumble upon you. Will you be kind enough to
name a place where you will be at fifteen minutes
before two to-morrow afternoon?   If you will, sir,
we will cancel this claim."

Mr. Barncastle said this with great dignity,
and drew his coat about him with an air of injured
innocence.

"Again," said Zach. as if speaking to himself,
"for the five hundredth time the man comes to lie
to me about that money."

"I will not," said Mr. Barncastle, "presume to
lecture you on your duty at such a time. I will
not enlarge on the impropriety, I might say,
cruelty, of permitting the public good to yield to
private greed. But I will say, Mr. Martin, that
it is your duty to look loftier. Drown sordid
Thought in the butt of patriotism, and rise to the
level of a statesman."

Barncastle's face glowed with such exaltation
as he said this that Zach. was fairly lost in wonder,

but his indignation soon revived. Turning round and facing that eminent man, Zach. thus addressed him:

"When I first came to Washington you took me in. You swindled me; you humbugged me; You got fifty dollars for doing it, and I am willing to pay you that much for teaching me the price of being duped by a great rascal. But I can't see that I have any further use for you, and I shall be infinitely obliged if you will take your leave as speedily as possible."

Barncastle rose with pride.

"Mr. Martin," said he, "I would call you my friend, but it might .be disagreeable—there is a chord in the human breast that needs but one touch to vibrate painfully. If you have touched that chord in this bosom —"

"Now that will do, Barncastle," interrupted Zach. "Will you be kind enough to get out?"

"Get out!" repeated Barncastle; "get out, sir! If my presence is offensive, you have but to mention it."

"But I have mentioned it," said Zach.

"Ingratitude," continued Barncastle, taking his hat, "is a sentiment unknown to the family of which I happen to be an unworthy scion. I can not, therefore, understand it. I shall take my leave, sir."

"Well, take it," said Zach., "and have done with it."

" It is probably useless," said Barncastle, pausing, "to appeal to you, but at this moment I am financially low. I confess it, and necessity, Mr. Martin, knows no law; it humbles the proudest spirit. Might I, sir, ask the loan of an X until morning? "

Barncastle struck a stage attitude as he said this, and placed his right hand in his bosom.

"No," exclaimed Zach., very positively.

"A V, then," said Barncastle. "I reduce myself to the ranks. A paltry V."

"No!" reiterated Zach.

" No!" exclaimed Barncastle. " You said no!"

"I said no," returned Zach, "and I meant no."

"Mr. Martin," said Barncastle sadly, but still with dignity, "good morning." He advanced to the door, but turned before opening it, and continued. "I would say, because hunger is even more potent than pride, I would say, and I will say, two dollars."

"I told you *no*," returned Zach., again.

"I know it," said Barncastle; "I heard the sharp reply, but a heart shrouded in misery does not heed, with that natural indignation which would otherwise be aroused, these rebuffs of proud men."

"Well, *you* may heed them," said Zach. "Once more I tell you *no*."

"Mr. Martin," said Barncastle. "I bid you good morning, and may you never know the pangs of a proud heart touched by the icy hand of indigence. Would it be too much to say one dollar. A hundred cents."

"Not a cent," said Zach. resolutely.

"Mr. Martin," said Barncastle with his hand

upon the door, "good morning," and at last he was gone.

Zach. drew a sigh of relief. "The scoundrel," said he. "To think, now, of the intimate friend of the President being reduced to such a strait!" He was settling himself in his chair once more, when the door opened slightly and Barncastle stuck his head through the aperture.

"Fifty cents!" he ejaculated.

"No, sir," exclaimed Zach., turning round quickly, "I have told you a dozen times, no."

Barncastle drew the door partly together, and said, with a look and tone that was really pathetic —

"A dime, Martin. Ten cents."

There was something in his face that someway made Zach. at last hesitate. His resolution deserted him. With that sudden impulse which frequently overcomes men of warm hearts, he told Barncastle to come in. The latter obeyed, looking exceedingly downcast and humble.

"There never was anything like it," said Zach.,

and he put his hand in his pocket and took out a roll of bills. Thoroughly angry with himself and with Barncastle, he selected a ten dollar note and handed it to the latter. "There, you incorrigible bore," said he, "take that, and now I tell you plainly if you ever ask me for another cent I will cane you within an inch of your life. Now, get out."

As Barncastle clutched the note his eye brightened, and his form grew erect and elastic. The humility was gone in an instant, and the old grandiloquent air returned.

"Noble philanthropist, generous-hearted statesman," he exclaimed.

"Go," thundered Zach. "before I kick you out."

Barncastle started toward the door, but as he turned the knob he waved his hand majestically. "Friend of stricken genius," said he, "consider this loaned for a day; I shall ——." But Zach. made a threatening movement, and Barncastle disappeared through the door, throwing back a last "good morning!"

CHAPTER XVIII.

MISS CRISTOPHER GIVES ZACH. A SURPRISE.

That night there was a distinguished gathering at the Arlington House parlors. The portrait that was to be exhibited was hung at one end, carefully concealed by red drapery, where it awaited unveiling. Zach. had called at an early hour for Belle, and not finding her ready had strolled out for half an hour. While he was absent a singular scene was being enacted in the house of the Marmalukes. Belle stood with her hat and shawl on awaiting Zach.'s appearance, while Hartwell was leaning over the back of a chair speaking earnestly to her.

"So you really think he will be defeated?" said Belle.

"As certain as the sun shines," replied Hartwell. "You asked him to make that appointment and he did it."

"Well."

"He had no business to do it, but that is not all. He is accused in his district of being bribed to do it. I have attended to that, and with the other charges against him he can not be renominated." ˙

"It was a pity to defeat him so soon," said Belle, musingly.

"So soon!" repeated Hartwell.

"Yes," returned Belle; "it's delightful having these men spending their money so freely on one."

"I suppose so," said Hartwell; "but I am tired of waiting."

"Well, what better are you off?" she returned. "Ma will never consent to my marrying you. You have no money, and I must have money. You have no position, and ma insists upon position."

"I am not so poor as you think," said Hartwell. "You asked him to assist me, and he did it better than he thought."

12

" How ? "

"With his eyes shut, like the fool he is. I never told you the particulars for reasons of my own. But his father sent him seven thousand dollars to invest in government bonds. He thought the stock of our insurance company better, and so he invested in it."

"Yes, I knew all that."

" So you did; but the company is worth nothing; it is about to suspend. The money, however, will be safe enough." Hartwell said this with a knowing smile that Belle understood.

" Shame on you !" said she, playfully.

" That's not all," continued Hartwell, triumphantly. "He indorsed a note for a *friend* of mine for ten thousand dollars. The note was discounted at the bank, and unfortunately the *friend* has failed — Martin will have to pay it."

"Oh, you wicked man," said Belle, striking him with her fan.

"And last," continued Hartwell, " he has five thousand dollars in the bonds of our company in his possession which were delivered to him by one who will swear, if necessary, that he took them as a bribe for making that appointment of yours."

"I never heard anything about that," said Belle, "and you know he had no such inducement."

"What is the difference if appearances are against him," responded Hartwell, eagerly. "Anyhow, I can tell you that I have fifteen thousand dollars as the result of my last few years' speculation, and now I want this thing broken off and Martin given to understand that his visits are no longer acceptable."

"Why, fifteen thousand dollars will not be enough for us," said Belle.

Hartwell looked displeased.

"You are trifling," said he.

"Well," exclaimed Belle, shrugging her shoulders, "we will wait awhile, and if it all comes out as you say, perhaps ma will consent, but let us go on for a while and see what will happen."

Hartwell was about to reply, when the door bell rang.

" There he is," said Belle. " He must not see you here. Go down the back stairs, and come again and we will talk it over." The hall door opened to admit Zach. as Hartwell hurriedly kissed Belle and passed out as directed.

"Ah!" said she to Zach. as he entered the parlor, "I thought you would never come."

"I have been here before," said Zach ; "but it is not late. A little while, Belle, and we will not be waiting for each other in this manner, for we shall be always together."

"Like two doves in a cote by themselves," responded Belle. "Oh, that will be delightful!"

Something in her tones grated upon Zach. "What is it about the girl I can not fathom," he thought. "She is very beautiful, and that she loves me I do not doubt, and yet I can not understand her."

" Belle, you love me, do you not?" he said, taking her hand in his.

"Why, what a question!" said Belle. " Of course I do."

"And are willing to go through life with me, for better or for worse?"

"Ah," said she, turning her lustrous eyes upon him. "You do not know a true woman's heart if you imagine that she who leans fondly upon the man she loves in prosperity will not cling to him closer than a brother in adversity."

She said this very tenderly, and placed her hands confidingly on his arm.

"Thank you for that," said Zach., and he pressed a kiss on the upturned face, where the kiss of another was hardly dry. Then the two went out together.

*　　*　　*　　*　　*

The company at the Arlington, as before stated, was a distinguished one, though it numbered among it a number who could lay no claim to eminence. Among them were Mrs. Barker, Mr. Audley, Mrs. Sampson, and others whom we have met before.

They were chatting gayly, waiting for the cere-

mony to take place, the conversation as usual
being very light and unimportant.

"Now you can see what it is," said Judge
Spalding, "to be born lucky. Why, there isn't a
statesman in the land who would not exchange
places with this girl-artist; and, as for money,
why, her pockets are full, while theirs are generally empty."

"Not if half the stories are true," replied Mr.
Marmaluke, who, as usual, was close to the Judge.
"If we can believe the papers, we haven't a half-
dozen honest public men in the country."

"Stuff and nonsense!" cried the Judge. "The
papers once represented, that I had run away with
Tom Finch's wife, and Tom, who was in New
York, chartered a special train to bring him home.
He found that his wife was laid up with the bilious
fever, and hadn't been out of bed for a week,
while I was pursuing my virtuous duties as usual.
By the way, speaking of the papers—have you
seen those furious articles against Martin? They
tell me he will be defeated."

"Defeated!" exclaimed Mrs. Marmaluke; "Mr. Martin defeated?"

"Yes," returned the Judge, "they say there is no doubt of it. Oh, they charge him with all manner of rascality, and they say he dare not deny it."

"I saw some of the charges," said Marmaluke, "but I did not believe them. They can't be true."

"And what if they are not?" said Mrs. Marmaluke, tartly. "They might as well be if he is defeated on account of them."

"Marmaluke has got a fiery one," said the Judge, in an undertone to a friend, as he turned away. "I knew what she was and barely escaped marriage with her myself. Lord, how she would have warped my judgment."

While the above was going on, another conversation was taking place between Audley, Mrs. Barker, and others. Mrs. B. had seen the artist and was dilating on her extraordinary beauty and character.

"So beautiful and charming," said she; "such

artlessness! Why, in the few moments I saw her I felt hopelessly in love with her."

" Well, deuce take it," exclaimed Audley, "introduce a fellow."

" *You!*" said Mrs. Barker, looking at him. "Why, bless you, she has a thousand admirers already. Senators, judges, foreign ministers, and half the nobility of England and the continent are ready to fall at her feet. What could you do?"

" There may be that in my figure," said Audley, "in my eye, in my nose, that all the dukes and earls in this world do not possess. It's not an unusual thing. I've made many a conquest by the knot in my neck-tie."

"Well," said Mrs. Gammill, "if she falls in love with you — now mark!"

"Yes," exclaimed Audley, eagerly.

" If she falls in love with you she will observe you closely, in order that she may paint your portrait. That's the way these artists always do."

"I'll watch her closely," said Audley, chuckling.

" "But don't speak," put in Mrs. Sampson. "Let

your figure give evidence of the colossal mind that inhabits it."

"Not a word," said Audley. "Leave her in suspense, you know."

"Precisely," said Mrs. Barker.

"She's very beautiful, you say?" inquired Audley, anxiously.

"Oh, she has every virtue," replied Mrs. Sampson.

Grimshaw had stood by and heard this conversation, and muttered to himself, "Well, this artist is a fool or a paragon, that's certain. These women haven't accused her of a single crime." A few minutes later Zach. and Belle arrived.

"Mercy! what a crowd," said the latter as they entered the room. They managed, however, to move up in good view of the veiled portrait that stood on a raised platform at the end of the parlors. They saluted the acquaintances about them, and waited for the ceremony to begin.

"Are we not going to see the artist?" said Zach. to a friend.

12*   S

"I believe so," he replied; "but see; they are uncovering the picture."

The drapery that hid the portrait was removed, and the company stood silent for a few moments. Then a low murmur of admiration arose, which soon deepened into loud and continued applause. Commodore Grimshaw stood near Zach., eyeing the picture through his glass. At last he said, enthusiastically: "As perfect as life!"

"The expression is a little too sad, it strikes me," said a gentleman at his side.

"Not a bit," said another. "The President's face in repose bore almost a look of suffering."

"By Jove!" exclaimed the Commodore again, "the girl deserves her reputation. I would consent to marry her myself without seeing her."

"How do you like it?" inquired Belle, turning to Zach.

"Very much," he returned. "It seems to me perfection."

"Hush!" said some one at his side, "here she comes."

A prominent Senator, now no more, entered at this juncture with a lady on his arm. They came in by a door near the picture, and turned their backs to the audience as they ascended the platform. The lady was exquisitely dressed, her slender figure being set off to great advantage by a heavy dress of white.

They turned on the platform and her companion spoke: ·

"Ladies and gentlemen," said he, "it gives me great pleasure to present to you one whom we all delight to honor, and one whose signal genius is destined to add so much to our world of art, Miss Margaret Cristopher."

The assemblage broke into a loud clapping of hands, and the artist for the first time raised her head. As she did so Zach. started as if struck by a blow.

"Good heavens!" he exclaimed, staggering back and rubbing his eyes.

"What is the matter?" inquired Belle, stepping hastily to his side.

Zach. looked again at the stage, but the lady had descended and was lost in the gathering. Before they could make their way through the dense crowd that surrounded the artist she had left the room, pleading indisposition. Zach. stood, puzzled and irresolute. "It can not be," he said, "and yet the resemblance is perfectly astounding. I must see that girl again."

CHAPTER XIX.

IN WHICH ZACH. MAKES THE ACQUAINTANCE OF
MISFORTUNE.

Audley was charmed. He had seen the artist, and she surpassed all the praise that had been bestowed upon her. He recounted to the ladies his experience, his impressions, and his hopes.

"I was standing right in front of her," he said. "As she raised her eyes she glanced full upon me. I remained in my position immovable, but with my eyes speaking volumes. I'd lay a hundred to one she's struck."

"Oh, impossible!" said Mrs. Barker. "So sudden?"

"Why impossible?" responded Audley. "Have not thousands of people fallen in love at first sight?"

"Certainly," said Mrs. Sampson. "Who could gaze unmoved upon that figure?"

Audley simpered.

"Look at his boots," pursued Mrs. Sampson, "his gloves, his neck-tie — his whole appearance, in fact."

The ladies all turned their eyes upon him in silent admiration.

"Now, really," said Audley, deprecatingly, but well pleased; "now really, ladies, don't."

"Oh, you needn't deny it, Audley," said Mrs. Barker. "The more I think of it the more I am convinced the artist is done for. We who are accustomed to seeing you can not realize the effect you must have upon a stranger."

"Now, really, ladies," exclaimed Audley, putting up his hands, "I can't permit it — positively now."

"You never saw her before?" inquired Mrs. Sampson.

"Never," said Audley.

"Oh that settles it!" continued Mrs. Barker. "It's all over with her."

" Unhappy creature ! sighed Mrs. Sampson.

"Don't be hard on her, Audley," pleaded Mrs. Barker.

"For the sake of the rest of the sex," pursued Mrs. Sampson. "Promise us now."

"Ladies," said Audley, solemnly, "I swear— that is, I don't mean to swear, you know; but I assure you most positively the girl shall not be harmed. I am devilish wicked, and all that, you know, but this is a holy affection. I don't say that I will marry her, but, upon my honor, she shall be none the worse for knowing me." With this he gave an arm each to the two ladies, whose eyes were twinkling with merriment.

" Now remember, you wicked man," said Mrs. Barker ; and again pledging his honor for his good behavior, Audley walked away with them.

It was rather a singular fact that of all that city full of admirers Miss Cristopher became, before the week was out, best acquainted with Mr. Audley. Why, we shall see hereafter.

The very next morning after the scenes nar-

rated in the last chapter, Zach. received a letter
from his father informing him that the latter had
just heard from Peggy, who was living in an
interior city of Pennsylvania. She wrote, he said,
that she should visit them during the coming
Summer, and hoped once more to meet Zach. To
relieve him of all embarrassment she wrote that
all the old feeling was dead; that she freely
forgave him, and wished most heartily to be
friendly, convinced that that was the wisest course.
Zach. read this with a twinge. It was not so
pleasant to have her adopting his advice so literally, and he almost felt resentment toward Peggy
for feeling this indifference. He jumped at the
thought of seeing her, however, and determined,
he hardly knew why, to go home before his coming
marriage and meet her once more while he was
yet free. For the rest, he became so absorbed in
the contemplation of the coming convention, now
close at hand, that he gave no more thought to
the beautiful artist whose resemblance to Peggy
had so startled him.

The day of this important convention at last
came and slowly passed. Zach. paced his room
with nervous strides. A year before he would
hardly have turned his hand to receive a renomination. Even now he would have retired volun-
tarily with hardly a regret, but to be forced out
under charges — that was the rub. He felt sorry
that he had not returned home and made a personal defense to these attacks, but it was too late
to think of that now. He could only wait impatiently for the expected dispatches. It was nine
o'clock in the evening, and still there was nothing.
A number of persons had called and sent up their
cards, but Zach. was out to all visitors. He dreaded
to show his anxiety before people, and dreaded
still more the effort at concealment which their
presence would necessitate. It was nearly 10 P.M.
when a servant knocked, and entered his room.
He bore a dispatch, and Zach. took it with an air
of pretended indifference. The servant lingered,
and Zach. turned to him testily and told him he
could go. Then he opened the envelope with

trembling fingers. He dreaded to commence at the top, so he began at the signature and read it backwards. It was from his warmest supporter, and in a moment Zach. had mastered its contents and dropped his hands upon the table.

You were defeated on the first ballot in spite of all we could do. Those charges did the work.

That was the telegram.

He read it and re-read it. He was perfectly calm now. He felt disgraced, humiliated, insulted, but nervous no longer. He sat quietly, looking vacantly at the grate for an hour. Then he rose and paced the room, still thinking. At a very late hour he undressed and went to bed, and finally to sleep. When he awoke the sun was shining in through his windows. He felt oppressed, as if by some calamity, but for a moment he could not think what it was. Then it came to him, and he turned over and faced the wall. "It is the first blow that has come upon me, and it is hard," said he to himself, "for I did not expect or deserve it."

It might have been the first, but it surely was

not the last, as he was soon to find to his sorrow. When he arose and dressed he had a yearning to see Belle. She would cheer him and sympathize with him, and he needed some one to talk to.

"It's not all lost," thought he, with a sudden thrill of pleasure. "Belle yet remains to me. She has been my comfort in my success. She shall be my reliance in my disappointment. I remember her words—bless her for uttering them—'She who leans fondly upon you in prosperity will cling closer than a brother in adversity.' I will go to her. She will give me strength and courage to retrieve this misfortune." And taking his hat Zach. walked swiftly away toward the house of the Marmalukes.

While he was on his way there, another queer scene was occurring in the parlors of that familiar abode. Mr. Hartwell was there once more, and Mr. Audley accompanied him. It was not yet ten o'clock, but Belle and her mother were seated listening gravely to what the gentlemen were communicating. Hartwell held a morning paper in his hand, from which he had been reading.

"We rather thought it might be interesting news," said he, with a meaning glance at Belle, "and so we dropped in to let you see it."

"It's the strangest thing," said Audley, "but there's no mistake. Martin is confoundedly beaten."

"There's nothing so strange about it," said Hartwell; "others have been beaten before him."

"Yes; but Martin was so honest, you see," said Audley. "I don't know why the stupid people should want to defeat a man that's honest."

"I am sorry to speak a word against one who has been a friend to us all," said Hartwell; "but serious charges, and I understand, proofs, have been made that Martin is a dishonest speculator."

"I heard as much," said Mrs. Marmaluke, "some days ago."

"Oh, is that so?" responded Audley. "Of course he ought to be defeated then. But Miss

Belle there needn't look down-hearted; he'll come up again, I warrant."

"What has Belle to do with it, pray?" asked Mrs. Marmaluke, with some asperity.

"Oh, nothing, of course," replied Audley, "only I supposed they were—well, that is to say, engaged, as it were."

"Nothing of the kind, I assure you," responded Mrs. Marmaluke. "We have only received Mr. Martin as any other friend."

"Oh, that makes a difference," said Audley.

The paper that Hartwell had been reading from had an unusually lengthy "special" about the convention, and it set out the defeat of Martin in all its completeness. Zach. had not been simply beaten, he had been overwhelmed, and a person had been nominated absolutely unknown, even in the district, save to a very few. Hartwell and Spiker, with whom he co-operated, had looked to the matter of the dispatch, and had the charges set forth as the cause of his defeat with a great deal of flourish and detail. Mrs. Marmaluke's resolution was soon formed. She expected a call from Zach., and she prepared for it. Belle was instructed to write a letter breaking off the engagement, which she did then and there. Mrs. Marmaluke was about to send the note to the hotel, hoping thereby to avoid the embarrassment of a personal explanation, when the door-bell rang, and a peep through the blinds revealed Zach. on the steps. Belle thereupon hurried to her chamber. Hartwell stepped into the back parlor and closed the folding doors, while Audley and Mrs. Marmaluke prepared to face the enemy.

Zach. came in, and looking around while he bowed to them, asked for Belle.

Mrs. Marmaluke drew herself up rather stiffly. "Mr. Martin," said she, "we are extremely sorry for you, and, believe me, no one can feel this blow more keenly than my daughter. The poor child suffers with her friends always, such is her sensitiveness. But you will see at once that in the face of such plain and uncontradicted charges, it would be improper for her to continue her acquaintance with you. Circumstances have rendered it necessary that all relations between you should be broken off, and it is best that this should be understood at once."

Mrs. Marmaluke thought this rather neat, putting the charges and not the defeat as the reason for breaking off the match.

Hartwell heard the words from the other room, and rubbed his hands and showed his white teeth with infinite satisfaction.

Audley thought this rather queer talk to a mere acquaintance.

Zach. was dumbfounded; he could hardly believe his senses. He felt, however, that this was the mother's resolution, a resolution that Belle would never share, and turning to Mrs. Marmaluke somewhat stiffly, he said:

"I prefer, madam, to hear this from Belle alone."

Mrs. Marmaluke smiled compassionately.

"Here," said she, "is a note which my daughter has already written and was about sending you.

You will see from its contents that I only speak
her wishes."

Zach. opened the note nervously and read.   It
was a cool and calm dismissal, with only the com-
monest expressions of regret; as heartless a piece
of writing as could well be imagined.   He crushed
the letter in his hand and dropped it to the floor.

"And this is her constancy," he said bitterly.
"O blind fool that I have been!   The world turns
its back upon me, and she of all others to be
among the first!"

Audley, who had been standing silently leaning against the mantel, was touched at Zach.'s
manner.   He would really have liked to do something, but he had no judgment, no discretion, no
sense, in fact, and so his effort at comfort simply
amounted to an insult.

"It's devilish hard, Martin,' said he; "but
politicians must expect these things.   I ain't a
benevolent society or anything of that kind, you
know, but if fifty or a hundred dollars would help
you any, why here it is."   Audley put his hand in

his pocket, but Zach. never noticed him. Taking his hat, and turning to Mrs. Marmaluke, he said:

"I have no reply to make to this note, madam. It is perhaps just that this humiliation should come upon me, and I accept it. Neither you nor your daughter need fear any further annoyance from me. The road that leads by you and around you I shall travel hereafter, and as best I can, alone."

Saying this Zach. stalked out the door, his face flushed and excited. Belle had heard the conversation from the hall landing above, and she gazed down upon Zach. as he came out, hot and indignant. She thought she never saw him look so well before, and she felt an impulse to call to him and throw her arms about his neck and deny the cruel letter; but the feeling was merely a romantic one, growing out of the situation and not originating in her heart, and so she stood still, with a half-smile upon her face, and saw him go out from that house forever.

13   T

CHAPTER XX.

BOBBIN ATTENDS A PRESIDENTIAL RECEPTION.

Mr. Bobbin had been a good while in the capital, but had never yet attended a Presidential reception. He had often been importuned to do so, but there was something awful to him in the thought of standing in the presence of the republican court, and he had so far managed to escape the trial. But Mrs. Bobbin finally became importunate, and her husband was forced, much against his will, to consent to go.

Mrs. B. got herself up for this occasion in a style of magnificence rare to behold, and Bobbin gazed upon her with something akin to amazement. She attired herself in a thin white dress, upon which there appeared to have descended a perfect shower of pink ribbons. There was a brilliant pink sash around her waist, pink bows sprinkled plentifully up and down the skirt, pink bands around her wrists, and pink streamers in her hair. The latter was also set off with a wreath of flowers in which conspicuously appeared two enormous pink roses. Looking upon her, in what he flattered himself was a cool and dispassionate state of mind, Bobbin set her down as one of the most gorgeously attired females it had ever been his fortune to behold, and he looked to see the room hushed into silence when she put in an appearance.

"I ain't fit to be seen with her, that's the truth," said he to himself, as he sat gazing at her. "Such a woman ought to have a Major General, at the very least, to wait upon her."

However, there was no help for it, and Bobbin, in his best clothes, and wearing a very stiff collar that, being a size smaller than his shirt, gouged his neck in a very uncomfortable manner, prepared to attend her.

As luck would have it, Angelica, the small servant, had what she called a "'gagement" that very evening herself, so that the children had to be left with another girl, who was hired for the occasion at the moderate stipend of twenty-five cents.

"It's always so," said Mrs. Bobbin, who did not like the extra expense; "I never want to leave the house but that girl has to go out at the same time;" but she became tranquil as she surveyed herself in the glass, and finally departed with a smile of satisfaction.

The Presidential receptions are open to respectable people of all conditions in life, and the crowds that flock to them embrace the humblest as well as the highest.

Mr. and Mrs. Bobbin took the street-cars and arrived at the gates in the very midst of the crowd. The drive leading in from the street and up to the portico of the White House was literally jammed with carriages, requiring the united efforts of a half-dozen policemen to maintain anything like order. A perfect stream of humanity on foot also poured into the inclosure, and Bobbin soon found himself in one vast procession that marched toward the entrance to the Executive mansion like a conquering army.

Entering the spacious doorway at last, he was directed to the right, while his wife was bounced off in another direction to remove her wraps. Bobbin soon found that he was expected to give his hat to a servant in the cloak-room, and to this feat he applied himself with great assiduity. It seemed to him that about a thousand men were intently engaged in trying to accomplish the same purpose at the same time, and after a quarter of an hour he was no nearer the object of his ambition than when he began. Suddenly he got into a human current that set straight for the opening of the cloak-room, and without any effort on his part, save to lean back like a horse conducting a load down a steep declivity, he was hustled on toward the door. The pressure was so great that the crowd on either side of him parted like the sea before the sharp prow of a ship, and in a few moments Bobbin was clinging to the little counter

in front of the opening and handing his hat to
one of the colored men in swallow-tailed coats
who stood behind it. Having obtained his check,
the next thing was to get around to the door
where the ladies came out to meet their escorts.
This required full as much time and patience as
the former. Finally Bobbin resorted to a bit of
strategy, and succeeded. Taking advantage of his
thin figure and diminutive size, he dived down
amid a few hundred pairs of legs and came up at
last, very red and nearly suffocated, at the spot
where Mrs. Bobbin was waiting. Joined together
once more, the two then fell into the line and
moved step by step toward the door that led to
the President. Soon this line became so completely jammed and wedged as to make even a
long breath almost impossible. It seemed that no
sooner did the front of the line advance an inch
than the rear pressed forward two inches and in
this way the crowd became packed to a solid mass

"If I was out of this," said a fat man, whose
face resembled a boiled lobster, and whose eyes

were almost starting from their sockets, "they might take their reception and be hanged."

But there was no getting out.

" It's dreadful!" said a clerical-looking gentleman, who was pressed so closely to the fat man that he looked almost like a part of him.

" Dreadful!" gasped the stout individual. " It's horrible! positively villainous. What in the name of heaven do they mean by pressing so there behind?"

Just then a lady with a white satin train turned her head and said to the fat man: "I'd thank you, sir, to keep off my dress."

"It's not my fault," returned the latter. " They are positively pressing me *through* people."

"If I was a man," said the lady with a little temper, " I think I'd press back."

"Suppose we do give a heave back," said the stout gentlemen, and at the suggestion a number of persons attempted that feat. The result was that a lady just behind them, and who was immediately in front of Bobbin, uttered a cry, and in an instant more was leaning in a dead faint on Bobbin's shoulder. This brought temporary relief to the others, for a policeman shouted to the crowd to fall back, and after considerable excitement the lady was extricated and taken away. The gap was immediately closed again, however, and the pressure soon became as great as before.

"What the people expect to see, that they should go through this torture to witness it," said the stout man, "is a mystery to me. They can't all be as green as I am, and yet they come here to be murdered."

Still the vast crowd, some in silks, some in homespun, some in glittering diamonds, and some in gaudy pinchbeck, swayed inch by inch ahead. Bobbin never fully appreciated the luxury of room until that night, and as for Mrs. Bobbin, her temper, like her wreath of flowers, was terribly mussed and torn before she gained the inside of the first room. Here it was a trifle easier, and the throng went on slowly, until suddenly, so suddenly that they never noticed the fact until they were there—

the Presidential party stood before them, and the great pressure ceased—ceased so quickly that it seemed rather odd and awkward to have so much room. The lady whose dress had been trodden on, and whose face had been clouded and angry a few moments before, was being presented with a countenance wreathed in smiles, and looked as if the evening had been in all respects the happiest of her existence. Then came the fat man, and his visage also thawed out under the Presidential sunshine, and he remarked that if the crowd was an index of popularity the President stood higher in public esteem than any other man on the globe, for which he was rewarded by a smile and an extra shake of the hand.

There was one gentleman ahead of Bobbin who had suffered all the tortures of the occasion without a murmur or a look of dissatisfaction. He was evidently a stranger, and as he approached and the official at the side of the President asked his name the gentleman responded with a confident smile, "Green! my name is Green. I guess

13*

the President will remember me."   And he glanced toward the Chief Magistrate as if he expected the latter to fly into his arms with a wild cry of joy.

"Mr. Green!" called out the master of ceremonies, presenting the gentleman.   Green grasped the Presidential hand warmly, and looked into the Presidential face archly.

"Don't you remember me?" he inquired, with just a shade of disappointment.

"I can't say that I do," responded the President.

"What!" exclaimed Green.   "Think, now. New Liverpool—cars—two years ago—Green!"

The President looked at the gentleman doubtingly, and the crowd behind pressed forward.

"Please pass on, gentlemen, as rapidly as possible," said the master of ceremonies.

The President partially withdrew his hand, but Green persisted.

"I introduced you to the crowd when you passed through," said he.   "Don't you remember? Sent you my speech in the 'Eagle' afterward, don't you know?"

"Ah, yes," said the President. "Very glad to meet you again."

"How've you been?" said Green, turning comfortably to the side of the President and resting himself on one leg.

Green had evidently settled himself for a long talk, but just then, by some means, he was caught in a kind of human whirlwind which began spinning him round, and when he finally came to a halt he found himself in the East Room, and the path behind him blocked by the tide that poured through. So he subsided and began looking rather sadly at the portraits of the Presidents which adorned the walls. And thus were the hopes of Green, cherished for so many months, rudely dissipated. His services, his eloquence, his very name, had been forgotten. He bought his railway ticket the next day, and shook the dust of the capital from his feet.

Mr. and Mrs. Bobbin did not trouble the Executive long. The official herald caught the name imperfectly, and presented them as " Mr. and Mrs.

Pophim," and with a momentary clasp of hands they passed on and were presented with like irreverence for their patronymic to Mrs. President and other distinguished people.   Bobbin only had time to notice that the Chief Magistrate was supported by a formidable company of ladies and gentlemen, the former in a bewildering array of blue and red, and white and orange, and the latter in swallow-tailed coats and white neckties, when he, too, was swept into the great East Room.

Here the crowd was quite dense, but there was still room to move.   Seeing a good part of those present marching around in a sort of elongated circle, Mr. and Mrs. Bobbin fell into the current and were swept around also.   Bobbin was wholly unused to affairs of this kind, but he could not help marking the composition of the present gathering.   All classes seemed represented.   There was the "shoddy" man with his wife and daughters, all of them awkward and ill at ease, and yet brusque and independent, showing their ill-breeding by meaning smiles and smirks, and anxious to impress people with their great importance. But, alas, wealth was unknown and unrecognized there. Then came the faded belle, dressed with faultless taste, but showing the dreaded march of time in her features. She tried to smile in the old fashion that had won so many, but alas, the expression had lost its freshness, its charm had departed, and men turned from it with pain or indifference.

There, too, was the old dowager, bony, hollow-cheeked, and with wrinkles filled with powder and paste. When she smiled, the beholder looked for the plaster on the surface to crack like dried clay, and yet she tried to maintain her place with diamonds glittering at her skinny throat, with bright apparel, and, worst and most sickening of all, with corsage cut low, as if the shrunken and wrinkled form might still challenge admiration instead of pity.

Then there were bright and radiant girls, all happiness and vivacity, stately and elegant ladies in the heyday of life, round-cheeked and matronly dames, knowing their years and meeting them

appropriately and cheerfully.   There were high
dignitaries, low officials, foreign ambassadors, dashing officers, handsome clerks, country visitors, and
a great lot of bashful people, who slipped into
corners and were contented to gaze at and not
mingle in the moving spectacle.   Many of the
ladies had evidently come prepared, like Mrs. Bobbin, to excite the envy of their sisters by the style
or quality of their apparel.   But a large propor-
tion of them were soon content to stand aside and
envy others who far outshone them.   Mrs. Bobbin
really did attract attention, for her head, resplend-
ent in roses and ribbons, shone like an oriflamme
in battle, and her dress excited wonder, if not jealousy.   Detecting a number of ladies smiling quiz-
zically at her, however, Mrs. Bobbin subsided and
drew Bobbin into a corner, where she could see
and not be seen.   Standing thus apart from the
promenaders, Bobbin suddenly felt his coat-tail
pulled, and looking around beheld Angelica, the
small servant, standing before him.

"Why, Mr. Bob-in!" exclaimed that hopeful

young lady, grasping his hand, and placing the acute accent on the last syllable of his name as if to do special honor to this important occasion. "When *did* you come?"

Bobbin shook her hand with real pleasure. It was about time, he thought, that he was meeting somebody he had seen before.

"And Mrs. Bob-*in*," continued Angelica, holding her hand out to that lady. "How do you *do?*"

"Here's Angelica," said Bobbin, gleefully calling his wife's attention to the small servant. "Ain't that queer?"

Mrs. Bobbin curled her lips somewhat disdainfully.

"What are you doing here, Angelica?" said she, rather severely.

"Me and my sister—this is my sister, mum," said Angelica, introducing a perspiring young lady in a bombazine dress; "me and my sister, we come together—with Mr.—te-he—Mr. Phillips." Angelica turned around as she spoke, and introduced a very slim young man, with the lower part of his

coat buttoned so tight that it looked like a sur-
geon's compress to keep him from bleeding to
death.

Phillips bowed with great dignity, and would
probably have contented himself with this, but
Bobbin extended his hand and warmly shook that
of his new acquaintance. The two fell into an
animated conversation, in which Bobbin discovered that Phillips was in the hair-dressing line, but
had an ambition to get into one of the departments, a project which Bobbin promised to assist
him in to the extent of his power.

Mrs. Bobbin held very little discourse with
Angelica and her sister, and the latter regarded
her with considerable awe. She pretended, while
they were near, to be looking for some friends, and
once or twice turned to Bobbin and remarked that
she didn't see any of the "Members" that she
knew, and it was so strange that none of them
were there.

"I *so* much expected to meet Judge Crasher
and his wife," said she, "and Mr. Martin is such a

friend, too. I wish they would come. We might go in, then, and have a little chat with the President."

This had its desired effect on young Phillips, as well as the sister of Angelica, who were plainly impressed with the social eminence of their new acquaintances ; but the small servant did not seem to be affected in the least, and kept wishing they would begin to dance, while she balanced herself on her heels and toes, and now and then whirled herself about with an hilarious swing. After being assured that they did not dance at these receptions, she grew impatient, and talked about ice-cream and chocolate-cake till Phillips tore himself away from Bobbin and prepared to squander a part of his hair-dressing earnings on this wayward sister of his fiancee. He therefore wrung Bobbin's hand, bowed low to Mrs. B., and the trio departed. Angelica came running back to tell them, with many a snort and giggle, that Phillips was her sister's " young man," and that she, Angelica, would make him buy cake and cream till he "couldn't

U

rest," and then, when Bobbin was nearly suffocated with laughing at her "cuteness," she hopped away again, Mrs. Bobbin still proudly ignoring her, and gazing far over her head in search of "Judge Crasher and his wife."

A little later, and the scarlet-coated marine band began playing "Home, Sweet Home," and this being the signal that the reception was over, Mr. and Mrs. Bobbin departed, the former feeling that he had passed an exceedingly pleasant evening, and the latter disgusted with the whole affair.

CHAPTER XXI.

TROUBLE THICKENS.

"It never rains but it pours." There is no proverb so universally accepted as this. It was so in Zach.'s case. When he returned to his hotel from his interview with Mrs. Marmaluke he was handed a letter. He took it to his room, and, seating himself, opened it mechanically, his thoughts on other subjects. He glanced at it, and his face grew graver. He read it, and leaned back in his chair with a look of weary disgust. It was a notice from the bank that had discounted the note which he had signed with Hartwell's friend, informing him that there was a default in payment, and that the payees looked to him for the amount. It was a pressing case, and his first impulse was to see Hartwell. Fortunately, at that moment a servant entered with Mr. Hartwell's card, and Zach. told the messenger to show the gentleman up.

"The very man I wanted to see," said he as Hartwell entered the room. "This is very unfortunate," and he handed the letter to his visitor. There was a look of infinite satisfaction on Hartwell's face as he took the letter and read it.

"The very thing I wanted to see you about," said he. "I would not have believed it possible, but that man has decamped, leaving all his friends in the lurch. It will come near ruining me."

"And me, too," said Zach. "I know of no way to raise this money except by the sale of those insurance bonds. They are the property of my father, but I might replace them. What are they worth?"

A look of well dissembled pain and astonishment came over the face of Hartwell at this question. "Is it possible, Mr. Martin," he said, "that you are ignorant of the fact that those bonds are worthless?"

Zach. had risen, but at these words he sank into his seat again, very pale.

"Worthless!" he whispered. "And yet you prevailed upon me to invest in them."

"Believing them to be perfectly safe, I assure you," said Hartwell, "and regretting extremely that I was mistaken."

"There, go!" said Zach., placing his hand to his forehead and turning away. "I wish to be alone. If you are innocent, well and good; if guilty, may heaven forgive you."

"I hope," said Hartwell, preparing to retire, "that things will look better yet. I understand that you were defeated in the convention also?" He said this with a cruel smile, and with his white teeth glittering through the jet-black beard.

"Leave me," said Zach., not looking toward him. "I know the full extent of my misfortune."

"Perhaps not all yet," muttered Hartwell, as he disappeared through the door—"Not all."

Zach. told the truth when he said that this was the first serious misfortune that had come upon him. But it was certainly enough to have pulled down a braver man he. The money invested in the bonds, as we have before stated, was his father's, and it represented the savings of a lifetime. This was swept entirely away in an instant. The note which he had signed as a favor was left totally unprovided for, all the money at his disposal amounting to only a few hundred dollars. He thought of proceeding against the insurance company, and called on a lawyer for that purpose, but was answered that the result would be doubtful at best, and that the suit, should he commence one, would be long and tedious. When he paid the money out to Hartwell for the bonds purchased for his father, he had received a receipt, which he had mislaid soon after and never could find. He told Hartwell, and asked for a duplicate, and Hartwell promised one, though he assured Zach. that, having the bonds a receipt was of little conse· quence, and so it appeared. The matter had therefore gone along and he had never obtained a copy. Pondering all these things, Zach. finally strolled into his seat in the House. The busy hum went on the same as ever. A large number of gentlemen came to him and expressed their sympathy, but Zach. noticed that this feeling soon died out, and that from the day of his defeat he failed to be of much consequence to the members, to the officers, or, in fact, to anybody in Washington official life. The people in office from his district, and who had been kept there many times by his personal efforts, no longer regarded him the same. They bowed to him distantly, and letters began to appear from them in the local papers, signed "Fifth District," and describing the wonderful talents of his successor. There was one exception to all this. Bobbin stood true. He came to Zach. with the same great reverence as ever, but with a look of compassionate sympathy on his honest little face that touched the latter keenly. "It's not for me to say anything," said Bobbin; "but I believe you will come up again, sir, strong and pop'lar as ever."

But Bobbin soon had trouble of his own to

attend to. The new clerk in Washington who has political support withdrawn from him is in a bad way. If only the setting and not the rising sun shines upon him he may as well lay down his office. The ascending luminary has too many to reward with its rays, and a shadow soon settles upon the man without influence. Bobbin had offended Spiker by refusing to become a spy upon Zach. The official who presided over Bobbin's department had been given to understand rather earlier than usual in such cases, that the discharge of Mr. B. would be regarded with equanimity by the new member from the Fifth, and Bobbin was therefore overwhelmed one morning by finding a note on his desk informing him that his services were no longer required. He was stupefied over it, and kept opening it and refolding it, and rubbing his eyes and looking it over like a man in a dream.

"Pretty tough, ain't it?" said a clerk, biting off a sandwich, and wiping his mouth with a napkin.

Bobbin looked up from his chair and smiled.

"Why, you see, I ain't nothing to live on," said Bobbin, innocently.

"Nothing?" inquired the clerk.

"Nothing," repeated Bobbin. "If he would give me a month or two."

"It's no use," said the clerk, "I've seen lots of such cases. Comes like a flash of lightning."

Bobbin turned his eyes downward, and commenced re-reading his letter.

What occurred to him when he went home, it is needless to recount. But there soon came to him, as to thousands of others, the searching for employment, the tour of the government offices one by one, the inquiry, the petition, the denial. Alas, who can appreciate the meaning of this save the men or women who have themselves figured at one time or another as discharged government clerks? What a fortune the salary he had been receiving seemed to Bobbin. How he wondered why he had not managed to save up some part of that against this, his day of extremity. He had been so long a part of that great building, coming

14

in with its throngs in the morning, and going out
at night, that he instinctively wended his way
thither as usual, and when pay-day came around
and he saw the faces made glad by the receipt of
the monthly installment — to which he himself had
grown so accustomed — he stood almost like a
grieved and wondering child, whose brothers and
sisters have been rewarded while he has been
passed by. If merit had governed the action of
the officials, Bobbin would not have lost his place,
no matter how the Fifth District had gone; for he
was faithful and honest, and had grown by his
experience to be a faithful and valuable clerk. If
consideration for his condition had actuated the
authorities, he would have been given time to prepare for the blow, for such preparation was sadly
required. But Bobbin was only an unimportant
figure on the chess-board, who could be sacrificed
without inconvenience, and so the blow fell. The
very fact that he was so humble and non-combative
made it all the easier to get rid of him. The
order came from the chief official down through

lesser officials, until it reached the person immediately over Bobbin. Every one of these gentlemen was anxious to obey the command promptly.
The chief had political aspirations, and the incoming member might promote them. He desired to
placate all those having the ear of the President,
and this was one opportunity to do so without
cost to himself. He knew nothing of Bobbin personally; didn't even know he had such a man in
his department until asked to discharge him. It
was a very easy thing to do, and 'twas done, and
the member-elect notified that he could designate
another person to fill his place.

Bobbin did venture to speak to the chief of
his division about the matter, but the gentleman
smiled with such lofty compassion, and shook his
head so decidedly, that the former gave up all
hope before his request had been fairly preferred.

"It's no use, Mr. Bobbin," said that distinguished personage ; "no use, I assure you."

"Oh, I suppose not," responded Bobbin.

" Not a bit," continued the former. " The fact

is, hundreds of members are clamoring for places, and it's more than we can do to get positions for those with the strongest influence back of them. I'd advise you not to think of it. Good morning!" And he turned to his desk as if his conversation had not plunged the humble applicant into despair.

Bobbin tried other departments, but was received in such a manner that he grew utterly discouraged at the very outset, though he kept on until he had made the rounds. It was a singular fact that the worst treatment came from dependents like himself, and the lower the grade of the official the more insulting and overbearing his conduct. Going up to the door of a great secretary, he was intercepted by the messenger who stood guard on the outside. The latter was a fussy, important little chap with side-whiskers, a bald-head, and a very red face. Ordinarily he rose from his chair when visitors approached, but he had been mentally weighing and measuring Bobbin during the latter's progress toward him from the other end of the corridor, and he had made up his mind long before the visitor reached him that rising would be an unnecessary exertion. Leaning back and stroking his whiskers with his left hand as Bobbin drew near, the messenger looked very sternly at him, and as he approached closer held up his right hand with the palm outward, and beckoned to him to halt.

"Good morning," said Bobbin.

The dignitary in the chair did not deign to reply to this salutation, but said:

"What do you want, my friend?"

"I would like to see Mr. Heavysetter," replied Bobbin.

The dignitary looked at him very critically before answering.

"What's your business?" he said, finally.

"Well," replied Bobbin, blushing, "I thought I would see if there were any places—"

"There!" exclaimed the messenger, waving his hand, "that's enough. I know all about it. Dang me, if I don't think the hull country is a-huntin'

fur places.   What makes you think, now, *we* have
enny vacancies here?"

" I didn't know but there might possibly be
something," said Bobbin, meekly.

" Of course," said the messenger, "of course.
That's the way with all on 'em.   They think we's
full of offices—jest bustin' with 'em.   Wall, now, it's
none o' my business, but I ken tell you that you'll
run a mighty slim chance here.   But you can step
in that other room there and see the chief clerk, if
you want to."

The man pointed to another door, and Bobbin
timidly turned the knob and went in.   There were
four persons in the room—the chief clerk, who
was sitting at his desk, laughing and chatting with
a big, bold-looking gentleman near him, and two
other gentlemen, one of whom was sitting on a
lounge looking over a newspaper and the other
writing at a desk in the corner.

The visitor who was entertaining the chief
clerk was a well-dressed man, with short, black
whiskers and a very full face.   He wore diamonds,

and was evidently on the most confidential terms with the official. The occupants of the room merely glanced up as Bobbin entered, and then resumed their conversation without further noticing him.

The big-faced man was telling the clerk about the delights of his country seat outside of New York, and asking the latter to spend a part of the Summer with him. He dwelt at length on the boating and fishing, and from that they fell to the discussion of other matters, and finally to those of a confidential nature apparently, for they put their heads together very close and spoke very low. So it went on for an hour, Bobbin standing and waiting patiently for an opportunity to speak. Finally the big-faced man went out, then the gentleman on the sofa rose and presented some papers to the clerk. The consideration of these occupied a half hour, but before they were through with them in stepped a member of Congress who had a matter to present, and another half hour was consumed.

And so it went on until three weary hours had passed, at the end of which the clerk was unemployed and Bobbin approached. He bowed as he did so, though this hardly seemed necessary after being so long in the room. The high official never noticed the bow, however, but turned to his assistant and asked if "those papers were made out."

The papers were made out, it appeared, and were handed to the chief clerk, who proceeded to affix his stupendous autograph to them. Then he handed them back to the young man, and finally glancing up at Bobbin asked him what he wanted.

"I thought I would see," faltered the little man, "if there was any chance of getting a place ——"

"Did you write that letter, Billings?" interrupted the chief clerk, turning to his assistant. The latter signified that he had, and the official again glanced at Bobbin and ejaculated, "What?"

"I thought I would see," repeated Bobbin.

"Oh, yes," broke in the clerk. "Well, we have no places, sir."

"Nothing at all?" queried Bobbin.

"No," said the clerk, and turned away, while Bobbin silently stole toward the door. As he was going out he was nearly run over by a great, gaunt man, dressed in jeans and wearing a broad-brimmed hat, who came striding in.

"Who runs this shanty?" shouted the new comer.

Bobbin pointed silently to the chief clerk.

"Oh! you're the chap," said the visitor, walking up to the clerk.

The stately official made no reply, but cast a withering glance at the new comer.

"Are you the man or not?" shouted the latter.

"See here, my friend, I'm not deaf," said the clerk.

"Then why don't you answer?" said Broadbrim.

"What's the matter? what do you want?" inquired the clerk, testily.

14*   V

"That's the talk," said the stranger; "now that sounds like business. Wall, I've sent a boy up here twice for the documents on that Injun business. My name's Peters. Every time the boy comes back he says they ain't ready. Now what I want to know is, why ain't they ready? what keeps them from being ready?"

"Where are those papers, Billings?" said the chief clerk, turning to his assistant.

"I believe Merrill has them," replied Billings.

"Who's Merrill, and what's Merrill doing with 'em?" exclaimed the stranger.

"You go down and see," said the chief clerk to Billings, and the latter went out. Presently he returned with a big envelope, and placed it on the chief clerk's desk. The latter looked over the papers in it and then handed them to the stranger.

"Are they all right?" said the latter.

"Yes," replied the chief clerk.

"Humph! that's business," exclaimed the gaunt man, putting them in his pocket. "Yew kin do things brisk enough when **yew** try. What ye want is stirring up a little. I'll be dog goned if I wouldn't stir ye, too, if I wur here awhile. I'd make the musty skeletons in this 'ere dead-house jine in a reg'lar war dance. Bet yer life." And the lean man turned round and winked at Bobbin, who stood almost speechless with wonder at the stranger's temerity,

"Now I don't want to hear any more," said the clerk, flushing up.

"Oh, yew don't!" exclaimed the stranger. "Wall, I'm sorry fur that, fur I sort o' want to speak. Do yew know, young man, yew wear altogether too many ruffles for a feller that's paid by the public to work fur 'em. Yew kinder act as if yew owned this place; as if yew hired the public instead of the public hiring yew. Now yew want to git over that, or we'll clean yew out o' here, r·ck and heels. Yew hear me now?" and the stranger looked very determined.

The chief clerk was thoroughly angry.

"Billings," said he to his assistant, "call John and put this fellow out."

Billings went to the door and returned with the messenger who had held the conversation with Bobbin.   When the stranger saw him he burst into a roar.

- "What's this banty goin' to do?" said he.

"Put that man out," roared the chief clerk to the little messenger, and the latter turned upon the stranger very pompously and pointed to the door.   The big man laughed at this again and winked at Bobbin.   Then he started suddenly toward the messenger, who scampered to the other side of the room as fast as his heels could carry him.   At this the stranger laughed again. "Come, sonny," said he; "come here, I won't hurt you."

At this the messenger gained fresh courage and advanced, ordering the big man from the room at each cautious step.   He was yet five or six feet away, when the stranger gave a bound and caught him before he could escape.   He whipped him under his arm as if he had been a bundle of dry sticks, and paying no heed to the frantic kicking and squirming of the little fellow, started with him toward the door. Turning there, he said to the chief clerk, "If I had yew under t'other arm now I'd lug yew both over and put yew in the pound." Then administering a sharp spanking to the messenger he threw him over on to the lounge and stalked out of the room, leaving the door wide open. Bobbin followed, and saw the stranger chuckling to himself all the way out of the building and even after reaching the street, where he at last disappeared in the crowd.

If Bobbin had possessed some of the stranger's assurance he might have prospered better, for modesty does not seem to pay in this world. But he continued to meet with rebuffs on every hand. He had a letter of recommendation from Zach., but this seemed to be of no use whatever. Zach.'s influence was gone entirely, and he might as well have presented the recommendation of a Hottentot.

One day he was met by Hartwell, who, after a long conversation, gave him to understand that

Spiker would secure him his position again on one
condition.   Bobbin was eager and almost ready to
accept the terms before hearing them; but when
they were made known he turned away.   They
were nothing less than the false and scandalous
defamation of Zach.'s private character, which he
was to compass by writing a letter, and which
Hartwell pledged him should not be made public.
Hartwell was not satisfied with defeating Zach.
simply.   He wanted to put him beyond the
chance of recovering, and he looked upon this as
an excellent opportunity for securing a rod which
he could hold suspended over the latter's head.
But Bobbin exhibited such utter pain at the mention of the price he was to pay for reinstatement
that Mr. Hartwell gave that up.   Bobbin might
starve — he began to think he would, indeed — but
he would do this a thousand times before lending
himself to such a scheme.   And so, tired and despairing, he tried again and again, only to meet
with constant failure.   The articles of furniture
which his wife had purchased disappeared one by

one to keep bread in the house, and still he wandered around for work. At last he secured the position of a day laborer on the streets, and gladly laid hold of the shovel to earn the means to live. He was unused to bodily labor, and it went hard with him ; but he never flinched. He even did more than his share, fearing he might be discharged otherwise. For three days he worked in this manner, but on the morning of the fourth, when he attempted, sore and stiff, to rise from his bed, he fell back, faint and with racking pains in every limb. The next day a physician came to see him and pronounced him ill of a very malignant fever. Exposure, anxiety, and over-exertion had at last done their work, and Bobbin must rest, whatever the consequence.

If the system which precipitated all this on Bobbin's head was to blame and is to blame for like cases of sorrow and disappointment every day, in heaven's name let that system be changed.

CHAPTER XXII.

MISS CRISTOPHER FORMS A RESOLUTION.

It was the studio of Margaret Cristopher, handsomely and luxuriously furnished. The artist sat alone in a great easy chair, a book lying in her lap, her fingers idly clasped together. She was beautiful. Not a word too strong had been said upon that point. She sat buried in thought for a long time, and then suddenly rising began pacing the floor.

"Will he never call upon me?" she ejaculated. "It is now plain that he didn't recognize me. How the old days came back as I saw his face for that moment! Days, before ambition seized him. Days, when we were children together, and knew no place, no enjoyment, but the dear old home and our own simple love. And it never can come again. I ought to know that, and be stronger.

But what is all this flattery, all this praise, all this grandeur, compared with the honest hearts, the loving eyes that greeted me then?" She put her head on the table and kept it there a good while. Then she rose and slowly left the room. Pretty soon there was a knock at the door, then another, and another still, and finally it opened and Audley put his head in. He looked around, and seeing no one, finally walked into the room.

"Here I am again," said he. "I can't stay away. My days are troubled and my nights are sleepless. They tell me a strange light burns in my eye. What if I should go mad and be put in a straight-jacket, and have my head shaved? It's no use; I must speak plainly to her. She has received me kindly; I may say, warmly. 'Come again, Audley,' said she, and I have come again. Shall I declare myself this time, and risk every thing? I believe I will. But what does she mean by harping on that Martin so much. 'Do I know Mr. Zachariah Martin?' I do. 'Is he to marry Miss Marmaluke?' He is, or rather he was when

she asked me.   But what was Zachariah to her, or
she to Zachariah? 'Oh, nothing, only she had
heard him spoken of by some friends.'   Well I
don't care.   Love conquers, and I've no doubt
that in her heart she loves me."   Audley was looking in a small mirror and smoothing his hair,
when he heard the door open, and, looking around,
he saw Miss Cristopher.

"I beg your pardon," said he, bowing and
blushing; "but you said 'come again,' and I *have*
come again, you know."

"Yes, so I see," replied Miss Cristopher. "You
are very prompt, Mr. Audley."

"Prompt!" he exclaimed, energetically.   "I
am so much in a hurry to obey you that I'd come
the next time before I came this if it were possible."

The artist smiled.

"Well, what have you got to say to me now?"
she inquired?

"Nothing," said Audley.   "Absolutely nothing
—that is—shall I, shall I speak it, Miss Cris-

topher, shall I give utterance to the burning words, shall I —"

" No," she replied, quickly, "most certainly not.".

Then smiling again she said, " It must be painful to give utterance to burning words, Mr. Audley, and I wouldn't; there's no occasion for it; besides, I want to talk to you a moment about another matter. You said Mr. Martin and Miss Marmaluke were to be married shortly. How do you know this? "

" Why, there it is," exclaimed Audley, brightening up. " I knew I didn't come here to make a fool of myself. Why, I came to tell you that they are *not* going to be married."

" Not going to be married," repeated she, eagerly.

" Not going to be married," he returned; "the match is broken off."

Miss Cristopher hereupon executed a queer movement for a renowned and dignified artist. She jumped up and down, laughed loudly, clapped

her hands together, and ended it all by exclaiming,
" Oh, crackey."

Audley watched these movements with a very
bewildered air. At the last exclamation he looked
puzzled.

" Eh!" said he. "What did you remark, Miss
Cristopher ? "

" I said," she answered, going close to him,
" Oh, crackey!"

" Crackey!" repeated Audley. " Exactly; that
means—"

"Why, don't you know what 'Oh, crackey!'
means, you dear man ? " said she.

Audley clapped *his* hands now. "She called
me dear," he said to himself. "She'll precipitate a
declaration sure."

" But tell me," said Miss Cristopher, recovering
herself, "why is the match broken off ? "

" For the best reason in the world," replied
Audley. "She refused to marry him, and canceled
the engagement."

"And why was she going to marry Mr. Martin at all?"

"Position, nothing else," returned Audley. "Why, what else had he? His figure is bad, positively intolerable, and as for his taste, I've seen him with checkered pantaloons and a striped necktie on at a full dress ball."

"Impossible!" exclaimed Miss Cristopher.

"I hope I may be struck dead if it ain't true," said Audley, earnestly.

"And so she will lose the position now," pursued Miss C.

"Lose!" he returned. "No, she'll lose nothing. His position is gone."

"How gone?" said she.

"Defeated!" said Audley. "Oh, he's nobody now."

Miss Cristopher bit her lip.

"And what defeated him?" she asked.

"Oh, they say he's a hard one altogether," he returned. "Guilty of bribery and forgery and murder, for what I know."

"Audley!"

The young man jumped as if struck. The word had been fairly hurled at him, and looking at Miss Cristopher, he saw her standing with her eyes flashing, gazing at him as if she would strangle him.

"Why, Miss Cristopher!" he stammered "Why—now—"

"Do not lisp such words again in my presence," said she. "I will not endure it. They are mean, contemptible slanders."

"Of course—certainly," replied Audley. "I only told what they say, you know, and he was defeated on them."

"Defeated?" she replied. "Yes; but a defeat brought about by slanders too base to deny and too contemptible to believe resolves itself into a victory."

Miss Cristopher seemed to have grown a foot taller as she said this, and Audley gazed upon her with admiration.

" By Jove ! " said he; "she's an orator and artist combined."

"Poor Zach. !" sighed Miss Cristopher, dropping her head and musing. " Tell me, Audley, for I think you honest—tell me frankly, do you believe these stories?"

" Do I believe them ? " he said.

" Yes; do you know any of them to be true ? "

"Why no; bless you !" said Audley. " I never saw the man rob anybody."

" But do you think they are true? " said she.

" Well," he replied, "everybody says so, and I have never disputed what everybody said; but I will if you tell me to."

Miss Cristopher turned away with a look of disappointment. " I'll not believe it," said she. "I'll not condemn Zach. unheard. I will see him and speak to him. If he is in trouble what fitter time to go to him and say, ' Here, Zach., as in the olden time, take all I have, and only believe that, were it demanded, my life should go with it.' He can not be so unworthy.   He can not have descended so low.   I'll know and judge for myself. From this day, Zach., you shall have a guardian spirit near you ; and God bless you, whichever way you turn."

And Miss Cristopher once more sat down at the table, and bowed her head upon her hands.

CHAPTER XXIII.

WHICH EXPLAINS PEGGY'S REAPPEARANCE.

It is time to explain the mystery of Peggy's reappearance as an artist, and under a name not her own. This can be done very briefly. When she arrived in Philadelphia she was very much frightened and confused, and hardly knew where to turn or what to do. She had discretion enough, however, to apply to a policeman, who directed her to a cheap but respectable lodging-house Here she found a temporary shelter and could look about her. She was advised to apply to an intelligence office as the quickest method of obtaining employment, and did so. There she sat during the greater part of two days among a number of rough and boorish girls waiting vainly for an employer. Two or three applicants had seemed prepossessed in her favor, but when they

15   W

found she was totally inexperienced in city work they passed her by for others. Peggy was getting greatly discouraged when, on the morning of the third day, a lady drove up, who seemed to be regarded by Mrs. Johnson, the keeper of the office, as a customer of much importance. She was a tall and stately woman, with a sweet and quiet expression in her face and with a smile that completely captivated Peggy.

"Mrs. Johnson," said the lady, "I want a good, competent, trustworthy girl for second work. Who have you got for me?"

Mrs. Johnson put her fingers to her mouth thoughtfully, and after a moment said:

"When do you want her?"

"Immediately," replied the visitor.

"I have no one waiting that would answer very well, I am afraid," said the woman, "but I can send one to-morrow."

The lady looked around the room and her eye lighted upon Peggy. Mrs. Johnson followed the glance, and said in explanation, "This is a young

girl from the country. She has no recommenda-
tions, and no experience in the city, and I suppose
would hardly answer for you?"

"What can you do?" inquired the lady, smiling
and addressing Peggy.

Peggy blushed, and ran over her housekeeping
accomplishments.

"Have you ever been out to service?" said the
lady.

"I have always lived with a family that took
me when a child and raised me," replied Peggy.

"Why did you leave them?" inquired the
lady.

Peggy hesitated and crimsoned. Her visitor
noticed it, and half turned away, as if she had
already abandoned the idea of taking her, if she
had ever entertained it. Peggy saw the look, and
nervously clasping her hands, while the tears
started into her eyes, she said:

"Oh! please take me, madam. I will tell you
the whole story, which is not bad I assure you, and
you need not keep me a moment if you do not

believe what I say." The poor girl had grown so
lonesome, weary, and discouraged sitting there
that she could not bear to see this opportunity
slipping away from her. The lady turned with
some surprise, and seeing the honest, truthful look
in Peggy's face, cast a glance of motherly compassion on her. Then she turned again to the pro-
prietress of the place.

"Very well," she said, "I will try her. What is
your name?" she inquired, again turning to Peggy.

"Peggy Clover."

"Or Margaret," said the lady.

"Yes, or Margaret," answered Peggy, though
this was about the first time this fact had dawned
upon her.

"I think we will call it Margaret," said the
lady.

"If you please," answered Peggy.

A few moments later the matter had all been
arranged, and Peggy with her bundle was being
driven away toward the residence of Mrs. Benedict. Mrs. Benedict was a widow lady, childless,

an invalid brother and herself making up the household. The brother's name was Cristopher, and he was a rather testy and very eccentric bachelor, ten years his sister's senior. He frightened Peggy very much at first, for he began talking to her in a very loud tone, and directing her as if she had been in the house for years, and knew every one of his whims and peculiarities. After a few days, however, she began to understand him better, and to regard him with curiosity and interest. Meantime she had told Mrs. Benedict her history, briefly, it is true, and that lady believed her, though Peggy insisted upon her waiting for a verification of her statement from home, where she had written, as before stated, and from whence an answer could soon be expected. A week after her arrival she was engaged one morning putting the library to rights when Mr. Cristopher entered.

"I was arranging the books, sir," said Peggy.

Mr. Cristopher rested upon his cane and looked at her without replying. Peggy kept on at her work, hardly knowing whether to do that or retire, when suddenly Mr. Cristopher blurted out :

" Peggy what ? "

"Sir?" said she, starting and turning toward him.

" Peggy what?" he repeated. "Your first name's Peggy. What's your other name?"

"Clover, sir," she replied.

"What!" he exclaimed.

"Clover, sir. My name is Peggy Clover."

"Clover!" he muttered, slowly and contemptuously. "Bah! dishwater; no name at all. By Jupiter," he exclaimed, after a moment's thought, and striking the table with his cane till it rang, " I'd rather have no name at all than Clover."

Peggy was much amused at the earnestness of the old gentleman, but she hardly dared to smile.

" No name at all," he continued. " If you stay here we'll have to change it. The Legislature can give you another in a jiffy. I'll get them to do it. We'll call you — let me see — we'll call you Shuttle-

worth or Patterson or Gildersleeve. Something
with three syllables. That I'm determined on.
Clover, bah!" And the old gentleman, with a
look of disgust, stumped away with his cane.

Peggy laughed heartily after he had gone,
almost the first time she had done so in months.
A few evenings after, she received a letter from
Mr. Martin, and went to her room to read it. Its
kindness, its almost more than fatherly affection
touched her heart, and the appeals to her to come
back to the desolate home made her very wretched
as she thought how unavailing they must be. At
a late hour she repaired to the door of her kind
mistress and knocked. Entering, she told Mrs.
Benedict of the receipt of the letter, and handed
it to her to read. Mrs. Benedict was much
impressed by the tone of the letter, and turned to
Peggy with even more than her usual kindness of
manner.

"He speaks here of a portrait of his son," said
she. "Have you it with you?"

Mr. Martin had alluded in the letter to the

picture of Zach., though not in a way to indicate
that it was her work.   Almost the last thing that
Peggy had packed in her little luggage was that
portrait, and it was now lying in her room.   She
therefore answered Mrs. Benedict's question in the
affirmative.

"I should very much like to look at it," said
that lady, and Peggy ran up stairs to get it. When
she produced the canvas Mrs. Benedict was very
much surprised.   She had expected a photograph,
but here was a fine, large portrait, executed with
much skill, and a wonderful fidelity to nature. This
much Mrs. Benedict, who was a connoisseur, could
see, though whether it was a good likeness or
not, of course, she was unable to judge.

"A very excellent work, indeed," said she
"Where was this painted?"

Peggy, blushing and faltering, announced that
she did it herself.   To say that Mrs. Benedict was
surprised would very faintly express that lady's
astonishment.   She questioned Peggy closely, and
when she became satisfied that the truth had been

told her, she regarded the young girl with positive admiration. Finally she asked Peggy's permission to retain the portrait for a while, and the latter consented, and bade her good night. The next day passed, and the subject was not alluded to. The next came, and quite early in the morning Peggy was summoned to the parlor. There she found Mrs. Benedict and her brother waiting for her.

"Margaret," said Mrs. Benedict, "my brother and myself profess to be tolerable judges of art, and we were quite sure your portrait was really an extraordinary production for an amateur. We preferred to exhibit it to experts, however, and have done so. They more than confirm the opinion we expressed. Now, my dear child, this is not the life for you, and we tell you so frankly. What will you do?"

Peggy nearly burst out into hysterical sobs as she heard their words, but restraining herself by a great effort she answered:

"I do not know. I am *so* ignorant."

15*

"I told you she didn't," blurted out Mr. Cristopher. "She don't know anything about it. We've got to take charge of her. The first thing to do, though, by Jupiter, is to get her name changed."

Mrs. Benedict smiled. "My brother and myself are willing to take you into our house," she said, "and provide means to enable you to pursue a regular course of study, only we, of course, did not know what might be your own desires or plans."

"Oh, if you only would," said Peggy, clasping her hands. "I think I only want a home and friends to advise me. I know Father Martin would gladly pay the expense of my studies if I asked him."

"But he shan't," said Mr. Cristopher, striking his cane on the floor; "Sister and I will attend to this business ourselves. You shall go to work here at once, and stay at work, by Jupiter, till you're a full-blown artist."

"Oh, how can I ever thank you?" said Peggy.

" By changing your name," said he. "Clover is detestable. I am morally certain that no human being can become an artist under the name of Clover. We can't get the case before the Legislature now, but we must manage it some way."

Mrs. Benedict smiled again at her brother's queer conceit, and Peggy, laughing, promised to think of some name of three syllables which she could tolerate.

The arrangements agreed upon were soon made, and in less than a week thereafter Peggy was pursuing her studies under one of the best teachers Philadelphia could afford. She made rapid progress, and in the Fall, partly on account of Mr. Cristopher's failing health, but more, Peggy believed, on her own account, it was resolved to spend the Winter, and as much longer as seemed desirable, in Rome.

Mr. Cristopher had come to regard the young girl with the greatest affection. He could not do enough for her, and it was to gratify him that Peggy consented to be known abroad, and professionally, as Miss Cristopher. Every morning, while they still remained in Philadelphia, the old gentleman accompanied his young protégé to the studio where she pursued her work, and would frequently spend a part of the day there himself, watching and admiring her. It seemed almost providential that Peggy had fallen into such hands. Both Mrs. Benedict and her brother were in a situation where any deserving person could have commanded their assistance, and where one like Peggy climbed into their hearts almost like an only child. They seemed to enjoy her progress even more than she did herself, and the consultations that they had, and the plans they discussed for the future were many and interesting. It was just after getting fairly settled down to her work that Peggy received a great shock. She had gone to her studies as usual one day, and had been particularly pleased at the warm commendation of her teacher, when finally, having finished her task, she put on her hat preparatory to going home. She was waiting for Mr. Cristopher who was to call for her, and who she momentarily expected, when she took up a newspaper, and ran her eye carelessly over the advertisements. All at once her eyes became riveted on a small personal at the bottom of the page, and she read the following:

PERSONAL. — IF PEGGY C., WHO LEFT HOME A few months since to come to Philadelphia, will communicate with "Zach.," she will confer a great favor and relieve her friends of much anxiety. Send letter to Continental Hotel for three days.

Peggy almost cried out as she read this, and started up as if determined to go at once to the Continental and answer in person. She stopped after she had risen, and slowly seated herself again. What ought she to do? She reflected, and then resolved to lay the matter before Mrs. Benedict and her brother, and be guided by their advice. She could hardly wait for her kind guardian to make his appearance, and when he did she met him half way down the stairs and hurried him away almost on a trot toward home.

"Why, what's the matter?" he cried out a dozen

times, as Peggy, in her great haste, shot ahead of
him, and left him struggling to overtake her. "The
girl is going wild;" and then he would take hold
of her and shake his stick threateningly, and try
to draw her into conversation and sober her into a
respectable gait. But it was useless, and Mr.
Cristopher reached home well nigh out of breath.
There the mystery was explained, for Peggy got
both of her kind friends seated, and then, taking
out the paper, read them the personal. As she
did so, Mr. Cristopher struck his cane violently on
floor, and blurted out:

"By Jupiter! I knew it! Yes," he continued,
"I knew it. I knew that fellow would come
mooning around here, sooner or later, and here he
is. Burn the paper up," said he energetically.
"Burn it up, and let me go and throw the ashes in
his face."

Mr. Cristopher was very much excited, and
Mrs. Benedict tried to soothe him. "It's nothing,
brother," said she, "only his anxiety to know that
one whom he regards almost as a sister is safe."

"Yes!" sneered the old gentleman. "Well, she's safe enough, and he needn't trouble himself."

"But what had I better do?" said Peggy, nervously, and showing plainly that she was half inclined to fly away to the hotel without stopping to ask advice.

"Let us reflect, my dear," replied Mrs. Benedict. "My judgment is that we had better send him a note informing him that you are in safe hands, and so set his mind at rest. If he chooses to call after that you can use your own discretion about seeing him." Peggy was prepared to adopt this plan, when suddenly Mr. Cristopher gave an exclamation. He had picked up the paper, and in looking at it discovered that it was nearly a week old. "Why, he's gone," said he. "Gone, by Jove, and we never knew anything about it. It's all up; the Congressman's floored."

Mrs. Benedict looked at the paper, while Peggy eagerly glanced over her shoulder.

"Sure enough," said the former, "he must have left town two or three days ago."

Peggy almost felt like crying; but as she talked and thought it over it became evident that it was better so. The result was that she wrote a letter to old Mr. Martin, as detailed at the time, which was received at home while Zach. was there, and which set his mind at rest regarding her whereabouts.

It is unnecessary to detail here the incidents of Peggy's life in Rome. During her residence there she became intimate with a number of prominent American families, and it was here that she first met Mr. Bruce, the young gentleman who finally accompanied her home. The portrait of the President, which was painted from photographs, finally attracted so much notice from American visitors that at their solicitation it was sent to Washington. Here it was received and greatly admired, and finally an order came for a much larger one of the same kind, and this it was which had been completed just prior to her return home, and was exhibited as before described. Old Mr. Martin had been kept fully posted regarding

Peggy's life and prospects after the first three months of her absence, and as he heard of her constant advancement he could hardly restrain his triumph; but he managed to say little, and occupied himself watching both the movements of Zach. and Peggy very closely. He knew the date of Zach.'s proposed marriage, and he had insisted upon Peggy's return a few months before that time. And so she shortened her stay somewhat and came back, arriving as before described. One sorrow had overtaken her and her kind patroness while abroad. A year after their arrival in Rome Mr. Cristopher had yielded to his many and long continued ailments, and after a severe attack had died very suddenly. He left Peggy a handsome sum in her own right, and, in case she survived his sister, a very pretty fortune. But Peggy's income from brush and pencil was now very large, and she gave little thought to her bright financial prospects. When they landed in New York Mrs. Benedict, Peggy, and Mr. Martin took the cars for Philadelphia, where, after tarrying a week, the two

x

former repaired to Washington, Mr. Martin leaving for home in high glee and hardly able to contain himself over Peggy's great good fortune.

It was shortly after his return, and upon receiving a letter from Peggy from a small town in Pennsylvania where she was visiting for a day, that he wrote the letter to Zach. which the latter received the day after the scene at the Arlington, and which convinced him that it was only a passing resemblance, after all, between Peggy and the artist that had startled him so. Having thus explained the mystery of Peggy's appearance and change of name, we can continue our story.

CHAPTER XXIV.

IN WHICH BOBBIN MAKES A LAST APPEARANCE.

It was in the afternoon, after her interview with Audley, that Miss Cristopher, or Peggy, as we may again call her, donned her hat and sallied out for a walk. She did not know where. She only felt that she could think better when she was moving than while pent up in the house. Once she turned her face toward the hotel, where she knew Zach. was stopping, determined to go in and reveal herself. But her heart failed her, and a thrill of pride also came to check her. What if Mr. Martin did not care to have her intrude upon him! What if the story she had heard was untrue and he was, after all, upon the eve of marriage with Miss Marmaluke! She walked down toward the hotel and neared it, pulling her veil over her face to avoid recognition. She gained the corner, and almost turned to enter, but wavered an instant and then passed on.   Then she walked rapidly, without noticing where she went. On and on she wandered, thinking of the strange fate that seemed to have brought Zach. and herself so near together once more, and was now holding them apart.   If Zach. had never been to her what he had been, if she had met him there in Washington for the first time, she would have passed him in all probability without a thought, and chosen many another in preference ; but the fact that she had loved him once and first, and the further fact that he had given her up when she was humble, though it mortified and, to a certain extent, angered her, made her, after all, ten times more anxious to win him, and gave him a value in her eyes immensely disproportioned to his actual merits.   She felt and knew this herself to a certain degree, but it did not alter her feelings.   We see many such cases in this world.

Peggy had been walking along for a full hour deeply absorbed in her reflections, when she suddenly heard her name pronounced, while at the same time she was pulled gently by the dress. She turned and saw a middle aged lady, thin and hollow-eyed, and dressed in that cross between absolute wretchedness and gaudy gentility so painful to witness, standing beside her. The woman's hands were clasped imploringly yet hopefully, and her dim eye brightened as Peggy turned.

"Is it," said the woman, "is it really Peggy?"

Peggy had not recognized the speaker at first, but when she spoke, her face grew familiar, and in a moment became known to her.

"Why yes," said Peggy, "and you—well upon my life, it is Mrs. Bobbin!"

She had hardly got these words out of her mouth before the woman had hold of her hand, squeezing and kissing it, and crying as if her heart would break.

Peggy finally quieted her, and heard, briefly, her story. It was as sad a recital as she ever listened to. Mr. Bobbin, after weeks of fever, was at the door of death. She had no comforts to give

him, and at length, after exhausting all she could
spare in the house to get bread and meat for the
family, had started out to seek help from the
authorities. Peggy turned with a full heart and
walked toward their humble home. She gave
Mrs. Bobbin money to purchase some immediate
articles of food and medicine, and the two finally
entered the house. Peggy looked around in dis-
may. The room where they stood was stripped
of everything. Two of the children — the young-
est—were playing on the bare floor, while an
older one was sitting mournfully by a door that
led into another room, weeping bitterly. He
wiped the tears from his face with a sort of dig of
his hand as they entered, and then, when he comprehended that help had really come at last, he
broke entirely down, and leaned over the window-
casing with great sobs that touched Peggy to the
heart. Then Mrs. Bobbin opened the door of a
bed-room and took Peggy in. On the thin bed
lay Bobbin, though she would never have known
him, so wasted was he, lying so quietly that she

thought at first he must be dead. But she soon noticed he breathed, and she sat down by the bedside.

"Look!" said his wife, gently rousing him. "See who's come, dear — one you used to know so well."

Bobbin opened his eyes, grown very large and bright now, and looked at his visitor. "It's Peggy," he whispered, and held out one of the wasted hands, or tried to, which Peggy took in her own.

"Yes," said Peggy, compassionately, "I'm so sorry to see you ill. I hope you will be better soon."

She held her face near his to hear his reply, which he tried so hard to make strong.

"I don't mind it," he whispered, trying his best to smile, and with the old feeling of regret at the possibility of his troubling any one. "I'm very comfortable, indeed. But, Peggy," with a great effort, and hesitatingly, "it's them, you know," with a glance at his wife and children. "I — I — don't

know what will become of them—so far away."
He could say no more, and tears stood in the
great eyes as he ceased.

"Please don't worry at all," said Peggy. " I
have plenty, and nobody but myself to look after.
I will take care of them, and I will take care of
you, too, until you get well and strong, and then
we will all go back to the old home together."

Bobbin heard her, and O! what a shadow
passed from his face as the welcome truth dawned
upon him. He tried to speak again, but he could
not. He hid his face, and the hot tears descended
and wet his pillow. And Peggy held his hand and
watched. As she gazed upon the wasted features
old remembrances crowded upon her. Some way
she seemed to be doing a service to Zach., to her
best of friends, his father, to all back in her little
country home, as well as to her own charitable
heart, by her kindness there. The many little
words of gentle compassion with which Bobbin
had greeted her in those days when, a poor neglected sprite, she had toiled in the little public

house in the village, all came back to her, rousing a grateful feeling, and making her present position seem only a poor return for his kindness. She had at first been disposed to censure Zach. for thus permitting an old acquaintance to die in poverty and neglect, but when it was explained to her that by Bobbin's express injunction he had been kept in ignorance of it all, she could readily forgive him. And so she watched.

In a little church, the rear of which came close to the room where she sat, some kind of religious services were being held, and the tones of the singers came through the open windows almost like angels' voices.

The song was an old one, familiar to Peggy, familiar to all of us, the outcropping of a great poet's reverence and humility, but Peggy thought it never sounded so sweetly before. And Bobbin heard it, too, and his face brightened at the sound:

> Come ye disconsolate, where'er you languish;
>   Come, at God's altar fervently kneel.
> Here bring your wounded hearts, here tell your anguish;
>   Earth has no sorrow that heaven can not heal.

16

Ah, Bobbin, simple, unoffending as you were,
what need you had of that consolation! The
words rang out clear and distinct on the soft Summer air, and Peggy pressed the wasted hand closer
as she listened:

> Joy of the desolate, Light of the straying,
>   Hope when all others die, fadeless and pure.
> Here speaks the comforter in God's name, saying,
>   Earth has no sorrow that heaven can not cure.

Was it so, indeed? Was there a Power above
and beyond the garish pretensions of mortality
that could reach down and lift this poor, unpretending, buffeted soul to a higher than human
level? Blessed be the faith that leads us to
believe so.

The song died away and Bobbin smiled, and
turned his gaze upward, as if he would penetrate
the thin veil that hid him from that great hope. A
look of peace was rapidly taking the place of pain,
and ere long he slept, or seemed to sleep, the pale
face, so pinched, and thin, and quiet, looking like
the face of the dead. They knew what was com-

ing ; the physician had left them no hope, and so they sat and waited—waited in the still hours of the night, and in the dull gray of the morning, Peggy watching and nursing, never tiring, never flagging. Mrs. Bobbin said little, but she sat gazing upon her husband with a look of helpless grief that was most pitiful. She was not intelligent nor acute, as the world goes, but suffering had worn away the grosser part of her, and touched at last upon true ground. And, oh! how her woman's heart went back—back to the days when, young and hopeful—for all have hope—she and Bobbin had started out upon the highway of life, expecting, foolish souls, to gather only the flowers by the wayside and make a journey of pleasure till they reached the end. And as she recalled this, into even her dim and clouded mind there came the bitter remembrances that press upon all, save the most hardened, who stand about the bedside of a dying friend; remembrances of many shortcomings on her part—many acts of unkindness, many instances of neglect. And with these came also the virtues of the sufferer, obtruding themselves, obscuring every fault, hiding every imperfection, upbraiding her for her lack of appreciation. It was too late to remedy this now, and that thought was the severest pang of all.

As the day crept in at the partially-drawn blinds, Bobbin turned his eyes upon Peggy, and whispered as she bent her ear, "You will help them, Peggy," and Peggy bowed her head, and promised; and then, with a smile upon his face, he slept again. It was an hour after when suddenly he awoke—awoke as if a new life had come upon him. His wife came to him, his children came to him. All surrounded his bedside.

" It's coming," he said.

"What is coming?" said Peggy, softly.

"The light," he answered, "coming so swiftly."

Away off—it seemed so far away, yet so near, it was so plain—a great light was shining upon him. The road was dark on either side, but there was the light, and its rays fell upon his face and lighted it up like a temple. And it came on, on, so steadily, so silently, so swiftly! Each moment its rays grew stronger. He turned to those about him, he heard words of tremulous grief, and then he looked again and the light was nearer. He felt his thin hand pressed, and was recalled once more to earth; it was only for a moment, but when he looked again the light was almost there. Then the objects about him lost their form, the features at his bedside faded into indistinctness, and the great beacon was shining full across his radiant face. His eyes were opened, but they saw no sight save that. His ears were unclogged, but they caught no sound save the rushing of that awful messenger. And then it was THERE, enveloping him like a mighty cloud. The unearthly radiance dimmed his eyes, and as it came and passed, poor little Bobbin emptied the sunshine of his humble life into the great blaze of eternity, and passed on with it.

O, beautiful Life! O, still more beautiful Death! when the golden sun of Immortality sheds its beams like this—a benediction on the dying.

*   *   *   *   *   *   *   *

An hour later and there crept into the silent house a small figure, bent and sorrowful, which glided with noiseless step to the room where Bobbin lay. It was Angelica. Her eyes and nose were very red, and she carried a very small bouquet in her hand, which she placed in the waxen fingers that were clasped across the breast of the silent figure. It was a trifling tribute, but it came from a heart as full as if the owner had been an empress. And then Angelica stuffed her apron into her mouth, put one hand before her eyes, and stole quietly away; stole out of your sight and out of mine; stole out of all chronicles forevermore, perhaps, and yet who shall say that in the great reckoning the small servant's gift may not be placed alongside many a grander one and not be dimmed by the comparison?

CHAPTER XXV.

IN WHICH BARNCASTLE MORALIZES, AND ZACH.
MEETS WITH FURTHER TROUBLE.

It was the evening of the 4th of July, and the
streets were bright with light. Rockets were soar-
ing, candles shooting, crackers snapping, and all
the confusion incident to the glorious Fourth was
transpiring in the usual way. Standing in front
of Willard's Hotel on "the avenue" stood Mr.
Ebenezer Barncastle. He leaned upon his cane,
and surveyed the brilliant scene with a smile of
satisfaction. "'Tis Independence day," he solilo-
quized. "Who wouldn't be an American citizen?
How we grow! How we spread! In 1776 the
common eagle, taking his flight from the extreme
limit of Eastern civilization, would have traveled
to the Western limit in a single day; but now the
proud monarch of the air, dipping himself in the

Atlantic, and then looking at the setting sun, ever intent and sailing forward, takes days before he cools his pinions in the sprays of the grand Pacific. *And yet* we are told that the people shall not be taxed at the rate of three and a half cents each for the celebration of the country's birthday! Despicable meanness! Intolerable greed! Why, for this our fathers went barefooted, and forded rivers with the thermometer below zero. Noble men! Unselfish patriots! There was principle, there was sediment for you. " Give me," said Mr. Barncastle, raising his voice, and speaking earnestly, " Give me a man with sediment in him! I don't care whether his hands are hard with dirty labor, or soft from playing the flute. What difference whether his breeches are baggy at the knees or at the foot! Who cares whether his shirt is cut bias, so to speak, or with a patent yoke and a collar? Give me a man with sand in his gizzard, with sediment in his maw — that's enough!"

There was some method in Barncastle's madness — rattle-headed as he was.

As he stood there watching the display, he felt himself touched upon the arm, and looking round saw Hartwell.

"Fine sight," said the latter, looking up into the lurid sky.

"Gorgeous," exclaimed Barncastle. "Observe the ambitious rocket. How it goes up with a roar and a hiss, with everybody to watch and applaud, and observe how it creeps back silently, as if ashamed after all its sputtering to be found sneaking around the earth again. It always makes the biggest display, too, just before it falls, and puts out the light when it starts downward, so that no one can see its degradation. But I know it comes down, for a stick hit me on the nose a while ago. It was the remains of a brilliant soarer, but it only made me sneeze. Pictures of men, Mr. Hartwell, pictures of me."

Mr. Barncastle leaned upon his cane and cast his philosophical eye at an unusually brilliant display of colored lights in front of the Treasury Building.

16*   Y

" Barncastle," said Hartwell, "you remember those bonds."

The political. philosopher only looked at Hartwell and winked, which the young gentleman interpreted to mean that he did remember them most distinctly.

"And you can testify as to what became of them ? " said Hartwell.

Barncastle again winked, this time putting his finger to the side of his nose, a mysterious performance, which had no meaning to the uninitiated, but which Hartwell seemed to understand most perfectly, and to be entirely satisfied with.

" I may want to use you as a witness," said Hartwell.

" All right; all right," replied Barncastle, again putting his finger to his nose and looking preternaturally wise. " You know where I am, eh ? "

And winking again, this time in a most diabolical manner, he seized his cane by both hands, leaned up against a lamp-post, and leered knowingly upon Hartwell. The latter seemed well pleased, patted his foot on the pavement for a moment approvingly, and then, remarking that Mr. Barncastle would hear from him again, walked leisurely up the street. He had hardly disappeared when Audley, who had every indication of having drank a little too freely, accosted Barncastle.

"Where's Mizzur Hartwell?" said he, looking round.

Barncastle regarded the young man with lofty compassion.

"Wasn't Mizzur Hartwell with you?" said Audley.

"Yes, my unhappy young friend," responded Barncastle. "If 'twould be any consolation to you in your melancholy condition to know it, he was."

"See year, old fellow," said Audley, "I ought to know your face. What's the matter with you? What's the — what's your name?"

"Barncastle, sir," said that gentleman, with great dignity. "My card, sir!"

"All right, sir," said Audley, surveying the card stupidly; "all right, Barn-Barn-castle. Can you tell me where our carriage is, Barn-castle?"

"What's your name?" said the latter.

"That's so," said Audley, slapping Barncastle on the back. "Of course; you don't know my name — Audley — G. Henry Audley."

A sudden thought seemed to take possession of Barncastle. He seized Audley by the hand and wrung it with great warmth. "Glad to meet you!" he exclaimed, "Delighted! Take my carriage." Here Mr. Barncastle stopped and looked around as if seeking for his coach and servant. "Where are the rascals?" he said. "Upon my word, yonder they go whirling down the street! They must be drunk!"

"Oh, im-imbossible!" exclaimed Audley, solemnly.

"They *are*," said Barncastle, "positively. drunk. Never mind," he added, "we can go afoot like honest plebeians. Where do you want to go?"

"I don't know," responded Audley, taking him by the arm. "Do you?"

"Well, we'll take the avenue and go where we please," said Barncastle, and, linked together like a yard of satin and a piece of faded cambric, they started down the street.

"Stop," said Audley, suddenly. "Hold on, Barncastle. Here comes a friend of mine."

As he spoke Barncastle looked ahead and perceived Zach. approaching them. He had his head bent downward, his eyes were upon the ground, and he hurried along as if eager to get out of the glare and tumult.

"Hello, old boy," said Audley, intercepting him. "How are you? How's everything?"

Zach. stopped, evidently far from pleased at the encounter, but submitting *per force*.

"This here," said Audley, tugging at Barncastle, "is my friend — my intimate friend, Colonel, Colonel —What is it now (hic), eh?"

"I have the pleasure of knowing Mr. Martin,"

said Barncastle, putting out his hand with a mix-ture of cordiality and reserve.

Zach. took his hand. "So you have," he said. "Well, Barncastle, there are bigger scoundrels than you in Washington. You take a man's money, but they steal his honor and his reputation. By the side of a stealthy slanderer and liar, you're a saint."

Barncastle was evidently troubled for fear Audley would gain a bad impression of him, and he winked to Zach. as he replied: "We have had our disagreements, Mr. Martin, but on the whole I believe we have treated each other honorably. I am sure that for my part I can speak nothing but praise of you to our mutual friend Audley."

"You're both good fellers," said Audley, ener-getically; "both of you—le's be friends—all of us."

"Martin," said Barncastle, extending his hand, "I forgive you—I forget everything. Let us, in obedience to our mutual friend's injunction, cry quits and begin anew."

Zach. thought the proposition rather cool, considering the circumstances, but Audley was enthusiastic over the proposition. He seemed to think he had healed an estrangement, and brought two old but alienated friends together. He insisted upon their shaking hands again, and blessed them as he saw their palms touch.

"Now, come on," said he, triumphantly. "Now it's all made up—le's go and watch the (hic) rockets."

Zach. was about to excuse himself, when Barncastle interrupted. "Stop," said he, "let me call a carriage. Come home with me and have a glass of wine."

He began fumbling in his pockets. "How unfortunate," he exclaimed. "I must have left my portmonnaie at home. My dear Audley, might I ask the loan of a five until I reach the house?"

Audley put his hand unsteadily in his vest pocket and took out a "ten."

"Never mind," said Barncastle, "ten will do

just as well. Come, gentlemen, ride with me ;
ride with me."

He took an arm of each, and Zach. was beginning to expostulate, and to say that it would be
impossible, when a gentleman stepped up and
touched the latter on the arm. Zach. turned and
confronted a Deputy Sergeant-at-Arms of the
House. "I beg your pardon, Mr. Martin," said he,
"but I am directed to summon you before the
Select Investigating Committee, now sitting at
the Capitol."

Zach. bowed his head, and then said — for he
had had some reason to expect that he might be
so summoned : "Do you know if there is a charge
against me?"

"There is," said the officer.

"What is it?" inquired Zach.

"Bribery," responded the officer.

Zach. said nothing, but there was a look upon
his face which even Audley and Barncastle
respected as they stood silently and saw him
walk away.

CHAPTER XXVI.

MR. AND MRS. MARTIN PREPARE FOR A JOURNEY,
AND ZACH. HAS A TRIAL.

It was as much as two weeks after this when a letter was received at the old home from Peggy. It recited briefly that Zach. was ill and in great trouble, and besought both Mr. and Mrs. Martin to come on to Washington at once. It was the third day after the receipt of the letter, and John was at the door with the old-fashioned carriage to take them to the depot. They were greatly excited, and in deep confusion with their preparations, which were of the most comical description. Mr. Martin was sitting with his hat on, but with only one boot, and was gazing around anxiously for the other one.

"Where's my other boot?" he exclaimed.

"Dang it! I believe half my clothes 'll be left laying 'round the house when we start."

"I knew it!" said Mrs. Martin. "The man's had three days to get ready, and he ain't no nearer it than he was afore. And thare that poor boy is a sufferin' among strangers."

"These women know everything," said Mr. Martin, adopting his wife's plan, and addressing an imaginary third person. "Three days to start off on a journey of hundreds of miles, and not a soul 'round to see to the cattle or 'tend to anything. I expect to see 'em all dead and the house burnt up, more'n likely, before we get back. And yet that woman talks about getting ready."

"There's your boot," said Mrs. Martin, drawing it out from under a lounge, and throwing it across the room to him. "Now put it on."

Mr. Martin drew on the boot and stood up and brushed the sleeve of his coat with his hand.

"How you *do* look, any way!" said Mrs. Martin, surveying him.

"How I do look!" he repeated. "Well, what's

the matter with me? Hain't I in misery enough with this coat and these breeches on, without your harping about it? They looked plenty good for you once."

"Yes, forty years ago," said Mrs. Martin.

"Well," he answered, "I've kept 'em in a drawer and ain't worn 'em more'n twice since, and what's the matter with 'em? When I went away to New York alone, a while ago, they looked well enough."

"I'm sure I don't know," said she; "but some-way you look all out o' shape, kinder."

"Well, *you* look brisk enough," he replied, sarcastically, "so what's the difference?"

"I'm thankful that I do," said she.

"Yes, you'll cut a big swell," he returned. "You'll set the fashions, I expect. Come on now, if you are ready," and Mr. Martin gathered a big portmanteau and started.

"Have you got everything?" said she. "What's the camphire in?"

"Come on," he exclaimed; "I'm sweatin' like a porpoise. Where's the tickets?" Mr. Martin put down the luggage and dived into his pocket, when, having found an envelope, and opened and looked in it, took up his package again and started.

"Ah, this traveling!" he groaned. "It's the last time I ——" but Mrs. Martin gave him a push out of the open door and stopped his vow never to travel more.

As before remarked, Mr. Richard Hartwell was determined to put Zach. beyond the hope of recovering his former place ; but this was not all the reason for his vindictive pursui of the latter. Though he was anxious and quite determined to ruin Zach. irretrievably, he probably would have made no extra exertions in that direction after defeating him and breaking up his prospective marriage, had not another circumstance in a measure compelled him to this course. One step in wrong-doing generally leads to another, and it was so in Hartwell's case. We have stated that the charges of bribery figured very prominently in the convention which overwhelmed Zach. These charges could not stand long, however, without something tangible on which to rest, and so, when the latter's friends indignantly pronounced them false and demanded proofs, facts, suspicious to say the least, were adduced that silenced, if they did not convince, his adherents. Zach. heard of these direct charges too late to meet them before the convention, and, as before stated, the fact that any explanation would involve Belle in disagreeable prominence, operated to silence him, even had he been otherwise prepared to explain. Of course these charges at home came through Spiker, who really believed them to be true, though their truth or falsity made very little difference to him, so long as they answered his purpose. But such serious allegations could not escape the keen eyes of the Opposition, and so it followed that an investigating committee, before whom other cases of a similar character were being examined, were charged with the duty of looking into this also. They wrote to Spiker, and Spiker referred them to Hartwell; and so, one day, the latter, rather to his surprise, was summoned before the committee to give his evidence. Belle was also called upon, and stated that she wrote the note which Hartwell sent through Barncastle, at the former's suggestion and dictation, and that she really had no definite idea of what she meant by the word "consideration" used in the letter. She knew afterward that certain bonds had been inclosed in her note, and supposed it had reference to them. Thus matters stood when Hartwell was summoned.

In the meantime a curious knot in this conspiracy was being unraveled in an entirely different manner, and by persons entirely independent of the committee. When Barncastle and Audley saw Zach. walk away, after meeting the officer of the House, as narrated in the last chapter, they fell into quite a confidential chat about him. Barncastle shrewdly guessed that the case spoken of was the one alluded to by Hartwell, in which he was to play the part of a witness, and, winking mysteriously to Audley, he informed that gentleman that he (Barncastle) knew all about it, and that he was the only person living who could, as he expressed it, "break the gyves of slavery and set the captive free." Audley was intoxicated, and more than usually silly when he heard it, but strange enough he remembered the words, and in some way must have repeated them, for it was only the second day after this that he could have been seen walking arm in arm with Barncastle toward the studio of Miss Cristopher, and finally escorting that gentleman triumphantly into the presence of the lady herself.

*   *   *   *   *   *   *

In one of the rooms of the Capitol the investigating committee were engaged in examining the charges against Zach. . The witness chair was occupied by Hartwell, and the Chairman was engaged in questioning him.

"What did you understand these bonds to be given to Mr. Martin for, Mr. Hartwell?" said the Chairman.

"I would rather not state, sir," replied the witness. Here was an evident attempt to shield the accused, and the committee glanced significantly at one another.

"We must insist upon an answer," said the Chairman.

"Well, sir," said the witness, "I knew they were sent to him to pay for the appointment mentioned."

Zach. clenched his hands nervously at this, and bit his lips till the blood came.

"Mr. Martin states," continued the Chairman, "that he had only seven thousand dollars in bonds, and these he purchased of you, paying dollar for dollar for them. Is this true?"

"It is not, sir," responded Hartwell. "The bonds were obtained of me by another person, and I was instructed to send them to Martin, which I did."

"That will do," said the Chairman; "Mr. Martin, have you anything further to offer?"

"Not now," said Zach., very despairingly. "This investigation has been so sudden that I have had no time to collect my evidence. Mr.

Hartwell gave me a receipt for the seven thousand dollars, which I have mislaid. I told him of its loss, and he promised me a duplicate, but never gave it. If he had not been aware that I had lost the paper he would not have given the evidence you have just heard."

"Mr. Martin," said the Chairman, taking some papers from the table and examining them; "we can only judge by what is before us. We find the following documents in evidence: First, a note to you asking you to make a certain appointment, and evidently, from its tone, inclosing other papers of value. The writer asks, significantly, if the consideration is sufficient, and you reply in a note, also in evidence, that it is. The lady who wrote you that note, for whom the appointment was made, testifies that the "consideration" was furnished by another person. It is evident by her manner, however, that she expected to influence you. A few days after we find that you obtained the appointment. What was the consideration to which both the writer of the note and you allude?

17 Z

We have the evidence of Mr. Hartwell that it was twelve thousand dollars in bonds of the Nantucket Insurance Company. We find on the books of the company that amount transferred to you. You confess to possessing seven thousand dollars of these bonds, and have nothing but your own unsupported word to show that you did not receive the remainder. We are extremely sorry, but our duty is plain. The crime proved against you is punishable by the courts, which we leave to deal with you. As you know, the statutes declare that for such an offense a person shall be fined in a sum equal to three times the amount asked, accepted or received by him, and be imprisoned for a term of three years. This, however, as before stated, is a matter to be decided by the courts. As for us, we feel it incumbent upon us to state to you frankly that we must report in favor of your expulsion from the House."

Zach. sat silent and very pale. He was revolving the utter ruin and disgrace that had overtaken him. This, then, was the end of his bright hopes, his great ambition. This was what statesmanship had cost him, and while he sat there, came sounding in his ears the words of his father, uttered three years before—

"However bright the outside of this public life may look it is full of trial and disappointment, and it may come to you, Zach., it may come to you."

Alas, it had come to him, crushing him to the very earth, and still the threatening clouds lowered upon him. Forcing down his emotion as best he could, Zach. spoke briefly and very simply to the committee.

"I acknowledge," said he, "that the evidence produced against me looks positive and overwhelming. I would not have believed it possible that circumstances could so surround with an appearance of guilt an absolutely innocent man. For I *am* innocent, as innocent, gentlemen, as you who sit in judgment upon me. Heaven knows that I never had the remotest idea of such a crime —much less committed it. This man Hartwell is a perjured hypocrite. Aye!" said Zach., turning as the subject of his denunciation moved uneasily in his seat. " I repeat it. A perjured hypocrite; a man who has bartered his honor, his very soul, to advance some scheme which he thinks to compass by my downfall. Some day the truth will be revealed. Some day he shall stand out with his mask stripped from him, and his iniquity blazoned to the world. Be it a part of my task to see this thoroughly and completely done."

The earnestness and apparent truthfulness of Zach.'s manner impressed the committee deeply, and Hartwell seemed to creep into himself and shudder as he heard the determination expressed to unearth his rascality. For the time being, however, the case seemed ended, and they prepared to leave, all save Zach., who, now that the excitement of his speech had subsided, sat moody and despairing, gazing blankly at the wall. Suddenly the door of the committee-room opened and a messenger hastily appeared, who addressed the Chairman. A lady was at the door who asked to be admitted, and announced herself as a witness.

"A lady," exclaimed the Chairman, with surprise.

"Yes, sir," returned the messenger, "and she says her evidence is very important."

The Chairman looked from one member of the committee to the other, and then, by common consent, they all took their seats, and the messenger was told to show the lady in.

Zach. had lifted his head, as had Hartwell, at the announcement, and both sat gazing with curiosity toward the entrance. Before they had much time to reflect the door opened again, and there before Zach.'s astounded vision stood Peggy — Peggy as of old, a little fuller in form and feature, perhaps, but the old Peggy, in her simple dress and unpretending braids, her eyes full of tears, her face full of determination. Zach. looked once — rubbed his eyes as if he could not trust them — and looked again, and then forgetting everything else, his own peril, his great wrong to Peggy, the proprieties of the occasion, all, save the fact that she stood there before him, jumped to his feet, and gaining her side at one great bound, took her bodily, forcibly in his arms, and hugged her with an intensity that would have been ludicrous had it not been so impassioned. The committee sat amazed spectators of this scene, and wondering what it all meant. Peggy released herself as soon as possible, all but her hands, which Zach. insisted upon retaining, while he looked in her eyes wonderingly, inquiringly, appealingly.   Such a meeting after all these years!

"What does this mean, Peggy," he said. "What has brought you to me now?"

"Wait!" said she, hurriedly. "Another time and I will explain. Is it true that they are trying to convict you, Zach.?"

This brought the situation back to him. He had absolutely forgotten it in his great joy, and he bowed his head as he answered:

"They *have* convicted me, Peggy."

Peggy's eyes flashed. "If I have heard the story correctly," she said to the committee, "I can give important testimony in the case. Can I become a witness?"

The Chairman indicated that they were ready to hear her, and she was sworn, and told to relate her knowledge of the affair. She stated the facts very briefly and concisely.

"Nearly three years ago," said Peggy, " Mr. Martin through mistake, doubtless, sent this paper to me in a letter. It tells its own story, and I submit it for examination. It bears the seal of the Nantucket Insurance Company, and is a receipt by the Secretary, Mr. Hartwell, for seven thousand dollars paid him by Zachariah Martin."

The committee took the paper and examined it eagerly. "It certainly is an authenticated receipt," said the Chairman. "What have you to say to this, Mr. Hartwell?" The latter was dumbfounded and only hung his head. The Chairman continued: "This certainly explains the seven thousand dollars, Mr. Martin. If you had a witness regarding the remaining five thousand dollars we could rejoice with you."

Zach. sat, half stupefied, in his chair, but said nothing.

"If you will permit me," said Peggy, "I have another witness at the door.   Shall I call him?"

"Certainly," responded the Chairman.

Peggy went to the door and looked out.   Then she disappeared partially and appeared to hold a consultation with some one outside.   Finally she reappeared, escorting the smiling but stately Mr. Barncastle.

He came in with a great flourish and evidently in a very happy frame of mind.

"Well, well! this *is* a pleasure," said he, walking forward with an airy swing to where the members of the committee sat.   "This is an honor. Gentlemen! they may talk about the labors of a member being light and his pay excessive.   Bosh! Nonsense! The arduous service that you perform on an absurd stipend of five thousand dollars a year, excluding mileage, stationery, and newspapers, is astounding. Gentlemen, some of you venerable in years, all venerable in attainments, if I were called upon to express an opinion—"

Mr. Barncastle was going on very enthusiastically when the Chairman interrupted him.

"There, there, Mr. Barncastle! Never mind this," said that functionary. "If you have any evidence to give in this case we shall be pleased to hear it."

"Certainly," returned Barncastle. He stopped talking for a moment, but went to work very industriously shaking hands with the members of the committee, until he finally broke forth again: "Here I find you," said he, falling back a pace or two, and surveying the committee as a whole. "Here I find you organized, laboring for the cause —discharging the solemn duties of office, earning the gratitude of your constituents, seeking for the applause of the populace, meriting the favor of your countrymen, and challenging the admiration of mankind. A beautiful sight; an impressive spectacle. Egad! talk of us as they may, we

17*

deserve our honors; we do, gentlemen. If it were not for us, look at the country! Who would protect it? Who would preserve it? Who would organize it? and without organization, if you will permit me to suggest a few thoughts, gentlemen, without organization—"

Mr. Barncastle was again going on at a rattling pace and threatening never to stop, when the Chairman again interrupted him.

"I beg pardon," said Barncastle, "but my delight at meeting you, banishes for a moment that humility which becomes the humble witness in the presence of an august tribunal. Swear me."

Mr. Barncastle was thereupon sworn, and took the witness chair with an air of charming confidence.

"You may state, Mr. Barncastle," said the Chairman, "what you know about certain bonds of the Nantucket Insurance Company said to be in the possession of Mr. Martin, and numbered from three hundred to three hundred and fifty, inclusive."

"Willingly," answered Barncastle. "Gentle-men, I have rooms in the house of an impover-ished, but respectable widow lady named Dabster."

"Never mind that," exclaimed the Chairman.

"But I must mind that," returned Barncastle, with a charming smile of complacency, "in order that you may mind what I am about to say."

"Well, go on," returned the Chairman.

"One evening, Dabster ushered into my pres-ence a gentleman by the name of Hartwell. From the expression of his back," said Barncastle, gazing over into the corner, "and you know backs have a certain expression, I should say that the gentle-man yonder, who seems to be chewing his tooth-pick, is the same man. He came, he said, knowing my influence and extensive acquaintance with members of Congress, to consult me about an appointment. He asked me as to the first neces-sary step. 'Mr. Hartwell,' I answered, 'the experi-ence of many years has taught me that the first thing to do in such cases is to organize!' Organi-zation, if you will permit me, gentlemen, is the first thing to be considered in any enterprise. If you are going to build a railroad, tunnel a mountain, build a ship-canal, obtain a land grant, conquer a difficulty, or celebrate a triumph, you must organize. Organization, I insist —"

" Mr. Barncastle," said the Chairman, " will you please confine yourself to the evidence in this case?"

"Certainly," he replied; "forgive the temporary digression. To summarize, Mr. Hartwell employed me as a sort of attorney to present Mr. Martin a letter and at the same time five thousand dollars in bonds of the Nantucket Insurance Company."

"And you presented them?" queried the Chairman.

" I did not," said Mr. Barncastle, emphatically. "At least not the bonds; the letter I did."

Hartwell gave a great heave with his shoulders at this evidence, while Zach., for the first time, raised his head.

"At first blush," continued Barncastle, "it occurred to me that I might do so without violating my sense of honor ; but there was a latent fear of bribery lurking in my bosom, and I spurned the temptation. I continued to reside beneath the humble roof of Dabster, pure as when I first entered that abode of molasses and innocence."

"You returned the bonds, then ?" inquired the Chairman.

"I did not," replied Barncastle once more, emphatically. "Regarding them as contraband of war, I confiscated them. I offered them as collateral several times, but, gentlemen, those bonds were glittering baubles. I tried to sell them, determined to turn the proceeds over to the public treasury, but they were worth less in the market than an ordinary I O U. Finally they all settled into my hands, and here before this august tribunal I now produce them."

Barncastle reached behind, and took from the tail of his coat a package, and, rising, said with a tragic air :

"Behold the missing bonds."

"There is no mistake," said the Chairman,

examining them. " They are indeed the identical bonds.   Martin, we congratulate you."

The committee approached Zach., and shook hands with him heartily, during which time Hartwell, with a scowl of mingled rage and fear, crept from the room.   Zach. received the congratulations of the committee in a sort of stupor, seeming not to fully comprehend the situation.   When they were through he sat down again, gazing vacantly at the wall, while Peggy regarded him from the other side of the room with a mixture of doubt and tenderness hard to express in words.

Barncastle was in the highest spirits.   He beamed and smiled in turn upon everybody in the room.   He took pains before Hartwell left to glow with satisfaction on that gentleman, and remind him of the "one hundred dollars additional" which he had promised the witness when the latter gave his testimony.   He received in return a scowl which appeared to please him wonderfully. In the hand-shaking Mr. Barncastle was in his element.   He insisted upon grasping hands all 'round, and took occasion to mention some little pecuniary obligations which he was under to the committee, and which he begged them to forgive and forget.

"This," said he, seizing the Chairman by the hand and wringing it till the tears stood in that gentleman's eyes, "this is a proud moment. In the hour of vindicated integrity let us forget and cancel all pecuniary obligations. Let us cast them from us as unworthy of us." The gentlemen said very good, and then all, divining that Zach. and Peggy might have something to say to each other which it would be embarrassing to speak before strangers, withdrew.

Still Zach. sat there, bewildered, thunderstruck, half unable to appreciate his good fortune. Back of it all, too, came the thought—piercing him like a knife and filling him with shame and penitence and humiliation — that here was the woman he had so grossly misconceived, so cruelly wronged, so heartlessly forsaken, standing between him and destruction. The pain was almost as great as it was a few minutes before, when he had sunk despairing in his seat, convicted of a felony. If Zach. had known it, the feeling was the best evidence of manhood that he could have exhibited. A villain or a fool would have accepted the service without a twinge.

Pretty soon Peggy crossed to where he was and crouched beside him.

"You need not fear," she said, softly. "I do not come to reproach you or to embarrass you. Simply to do my duty, that's all."

Zach. fairly writhed under these words. He struggled to conquer his emotion, but could not, and finally, losing all command of himself—man, statesman as he was—broke down entirely, and crying out, "Oh, Peggy! Peggy!" sank on his knees at her feet.

CHAPTER XXVII.

A WELCOME ARRIVAL.

Peggy's eyes were full of tears as Zach. knelt so humbly beside her, but there was a gleam of joy behind them like a ray of sunlight shining through a Summer's rain. There was a long pause, which was finally broken by Zach.

"That you, above all others, should have done this!" he said.

"Well, who had a better right, I should like to know, *Mister* Martin?" replied Peggy, mischievously, and laughing through her tears.

Zach. uncovered his face and looked at her long and steadily.

"I am utterly confused and confounded, Peggy," said he; "but tell me how in the world you came to be here at this time!"

"I came to Washington some time ago," she

A2

replied. " I knew you were in trouble, and I
found out the charges against you. I had intended
to be here earlier, and save you all this pain, but I
was detained. I found the room at last, and I —.
Oh, Zach., I came in time, did I not?"

"God bless you, my darling," said Zach., passionately seizing her and drawing her to him.
"Oh, Peggy! if you knew how utterly powerless I
am to express my gratitude!" And he seized her
hands and held them as in a vise.

After a while they began to converse more
calmly, and Peggy gave Zach. to understand that
she was serving in some capacity in a family in
Washington. She told him something of her life
in Philadelphia, though never hinting at her art
studies, and how she had gone abroad with a lady,
spending two years in Italy, at which Zach was
greatly surprised.

"When I came back," said Peggy, " I thought
I might as well work here as anywhere, so I came
on, and then when you got into your trouble —
why, I got you out, you know."

"And what a scoundrel I have been, Peggy!" said he. "Oh, I needed this lesson. I needed it. Can you ever forgive me? *Can* you, and take me back to the old place in your heart? I am poor now — but for you would be disgraced; but will you take me back?"

She was silent.

"If you can not," said he, "I shall wish I had gone down there an hour ago never to have risen."

Peggy looked up at him.

"You may not always feel so," said she. "You are in trouble and you are grateful now. By and by it may not be so pleasant to have an ignorant girl to introduce to your friends."

Zach. made a gesture of impatience. "Peggy," said he, "I deserve this; I know it, but there are some people in this world who are born wise. No lack of culture, no adverse circumstances can make them common or vulgar. You are one of those, bless your little body. I came to know that when it was too late. Let me tell you all, then judge me." And Zach told her all. He told her how regrets at breaking off their engagement came to him early and grew upon him all through those years of separation; how honor demanded that he should remain true to his new vows, and how he had tried to do so; how the letter of Belle discarding him wounded his pride, and, coming with his other troubles, deeply pained him; but that, aside from that, he would have rejoiced at such a deliverance; all of which Peggy heard and pondered, glowing and triumphant, but without committing herself in return.

"By an effort, Peggy," said Zach., "I can retrieve the past; with you the task would be easy. Say that all is forgiven, and that you have not forgotten how to love me."

Before Peggy could reply, there was a great commotion in the hall, and voices were heard expostulating with the messenger who stood outside the door.

"Well, send in your card," said the latter, "and if he wants to see you he can say so."

"Send in fiddlesticks," retorted a voice. "Dang

it, do you think I want an introduction to my own son ?"

Peggy gave a jump. "It's them," she said, trembling. "Oh, the dear old souls. Hear 'em !"

There was a word from the messenger about not knowing who the visitor was, and then the big door slowly opened.

"Come in, old woman," said the voice of Mr. Martin; "let's go right in and surprise him."

"Don't slam things 'round in that way," said Mrs. Martin, and then the door swung full upon its hinges, and there stood Zach.'s father and mother, their hands full of luggage, but their faces warm and bright as ever. Peggy and Zach. stood still in their places for a moment, and then, seeing them, the old couple suddenly dropped their bundles, " camphire " and all, and rushed across the room. In another moment Peggy was locked in the arms of Mr. Martin, while Zach. was closely clasped by his mother.

" Peggy !" said Mr. Martin.

" Zach !" ejaculated his mother.

And the door of the committee-room closed upon a reunited family.

CHAPTER XXVIII.

THE END OF IT ALL.

It was all over the town in less than twenty-four hours afterward; Zachariah Martin had been tendered the mission to Italy by the President. The conspiracy against him so happily defeated had given him the sympathy of his fellow-members, and uniting in a petition to the Executive, the appointment had been readily made. Mrs. Marmaluke had heard of it, Belle had heard of it, and the first movement on their part was to make an effort to reinstate themselves in the good graces of the "rising statesman." Belle had written him a note. It bore her monogram; was most delicately perfumed, and was written in the most faultless style. It read as follows:

My Dear Zachariah: What a mistake we have both made! I never heard of a more unfortunate muddle. We

were both deceived.   That all may be explained and set
right, come at once to your unhappy but loving   BELLE.

Zach. received this letter and read it with a
smile. He was just going to call on Peggy, who
was domiciled in the house of Madam Benedict,
and he put the note in his pocket. Since the
occurrence at the committee-room his ill-luck
seemed to have vanished. All was bright and
encouraging again. Not only had he been rein-
stated in public estimation, but his losses were
about to be made good through threats of a prosecution against Mr. Hartwell, which that gentleman had good reason to avoid. Zach. had succeeded
in conquering Peggy, not a very difficult task, and
they were to be married unostentatiously within a
week. She had been so careful, and had avoided
going in public so rigidly, that Zach. had not as
yet the remotest suspicion of her dual existence,
supposing her to be nothing more than the simple
Peggy whom he had always known. Once, indeed,
as she sat briskly sewing of an evening while
Judge Spalding and Zach. discussed politics, the

latter appeared to be suddenly struck with the resemblance he had before noted, and called the attention of the Judge to the fact.

"Judge," said Zach., breaking off the conversation, "did you ever notice how much Peggy and that Miss Cristopher resemble each other?"

Peggy colored scarlet, and turned her head, while the Judge looked a moment before replying.

"They do look a trifle alike," he responded with a twinkle in his eye, "but Miss Cristopher is taller and darker."

"I presume if they were together the likeness would vanish," answered Zach., "but I remarked it when I saw the artist at the Arlington, though I had but a glimpse of her, and could not judge fairly." This was all that was said, and Peggy grew easier.

As before stated, Peggy was domiciled at the house of Madam Benedict. She had informed Zach. that the lady with whom she was staying was the one she had accompanied abroad, and that she was treated as a companion and not

18

as a servant by her kind mistress. Zach. had proposed taking her out of her situation and placing her with some of his friends pending the wedding, but when Peggy introduced him to her patroness, and the latter exhibited such a motherly interest in the young lady, he readily gave his consent to her remaining. Indeed, Zach. was greatly gratified at beholding the consideration with which the humble Peggy was treated by her kind friend. He did not think it strange, for in his present mood it seemed perfectly natural that all the world should worship her; but it pleased him very much. Zach. began to feel a strong interest in Madam Benedict when that good lady, in addition to what she had done for Peggy, also insisted upon entertaining his father and mother while they were in the city, and concluded that she was the kindest woman in the world. He was surprised a little also to see how well the stately hostess and his rough and ready father got along together—coming upon them, as he did the first day of their meeting, in what seemed a very confidential and remarkably amusing interview which terminated at once on his approach. One thing annoyed Zach. a little, and that was the rigid seclusion of Peggy. He was proud of her, and desired to introduce her to his friends, but she absolutely refused to see any one save Judge Spalding, who was in the secret, and when Zach. appealed to his father and Madam Benedict to induce her to alter her determination, they both gave it as their deliberate opinion that it would be much better for Peggy to remain hidden entirely until the day of the wedding. Zach was silenced if not satisfied, and so the little scheme, which had been resolved upon, viz., to marry Zach. to Peggy without the knowledge on his part that she was any other than the humble girl he had known of old, worked very nicely.

Zach. took occasion during the evening mentioned to show Belle's letter to Peggy, and the latter was quite dismayed at first, but became reassured when Zach. wrote his reply and handed it to her. It ran as follows:

MISS BELLE MARMALUKE: Hard as was the blow that
canceled our engagement, I accepted it as final, and by reason
of subsequent events have been led to look upon what I then
regarded as a calamity in the light of a blessing. It has
brought, through seeming providential means, one to my heart
who ought never to have left it, and one whose love and constancy I now prize beyond measure. I take the liberty of
inclosing cards for an event which I trust may not prove unin-
teresting to you and your family; and have the honor to remain
your obt. servant,   ZACHARIAH MARTIN.

The cards alluded to were invitations to his
wedding reception, and Peggy's eyes opened pretty
wide as she realized this fact.

"Have *her* there!" she cried. "Oh,
Zach.!"

"Why not, if she desires to come? I should
certainly be much pleased to present you to her,"
returned Zach., laughing.

"But when you see her looking so beautiful,"
cried Peggy, "you may be ashamed of your plain
little wife."

Zach. laughed gleefully. "You plain!" said
he. "Now that's really good. Upon my word, I
hope she will come, in order that you may see me

under this terrible temptation; but I fear she will decline with thanks."

Now the truth was, Peggy knew Miss Marmaluke and her mother, having received two or three calls from them, and she trembled as she thought of the shock they would receive at recognizing her. However, there was not much probability of their coming; that was one comfort.

It was a few days after the sending of Belle's letter to Zach., and that young lady had not yet received a reply. She was considerably vexed at this, and her mother was on positive nettles. She inquired a half-dozen times a day if Belle had received an answer, and at each recurring disappointment grew more anxious. At last the postman brought a letter directed in Zach.'s well-known hand, and Belle opened it eagerly. She read it, and flushed crimson. She clenched her little hands, bit her lips, and patted her foot impatiently on the carpet.

"Peggy Clover!" she exclaimed, looking at the cards. "As I live, the ignorant country girl, of whom he was always talking.   Well! he is welcome to her."

Mrs. Marmaluke was excessively vexed, and high words passed between her and Belle, each accusing the other of being to blame; but Mr. Marmaluke happening to come in about that time, ended the quarrel, telling them there was no use "crying over spilt milk."

At first it was deemed absolutely out of the question for them to attend the reception, but finally fearing that their absence would be construed to the disadvantage of Belle, and that it would be better to attend and keep up the impression that it was she and not Zach. who had broken off the match, they resolved to go.

"Let him only see you by the side of the boor he has married," said Mrs. Marmaluke, now only intent on revenge, "and it will be triumph enough."

It was the afternoon of the same day, when Mrs. Barker, accompanied by Audley, burst into the house in great excitement.

"Oh dear!" she cried, sinking into a chair.   " I

am nearly out of breath, but do tell me quick are you going to the reception? But of course you are. It will suffocate me, I know it will. The idea of a girl like that the wife of a foreign minister! I presume she will receive in a checked sunbonnet."

"Have you seen her?" inquired Belle.

"I caught a glimpse of her," responded Mrs. Barker. "Her back is as broad as the Irish giant's. Oh, there's no mistake. She's a regular kitchen girl."

"It's the strangest thing," ejaculated Audley.

"I never can keep my face straight," said Belle.

"And you should see her shoes," continued Audley. "Nines!" He held his hands wide apart, as if to give an idea of the length of Peggy's feet, and then giggled excessively. If Audley had possessed the sense of an oyster he would have discovered something of Miss Cristopher's relations to Zach., but she had cleverly concealed her purpose from him, and he had not the remotest idea that she and Zach.'s intended

wife were identical.   Beside Miss Cristopher was
supposed to be in Philadelphia, and Audley was
industriously engaged sending perfumed notes to
an address which she had left behind.   He had
never, to his knowledge, beheld Peggy Clover, and
the joke about her feet had, so to speak, no founda-
tion to rest upon.

"What could have possessed Martin?" said
Mrs. Marmaluke, looking puzzled.

"Oh, I am told that he engaged himself to her
when he was down and in a fit of desperation,"
returned Mrs. Barker.

"Well, whatever his wife may be," said Mr.
Marmaluke, overhearing the last two or three sentences, " Martin has the position, and that's enough
for us."

"Of course," replied Mrs. Barker, " we must go
and keep our faces straight if we die in the
attempt.   But fancy that woman as the representative of American nobility abroad!   Enter,"
said she, placing herself in the center of the room
and assuming a comical attitude. "Enter his

excellency the Honorable Zachariah and lady for an audience with the King! They approach the royal person." Here Mrs. Barker stamped with heavy tread down the center of the parlor and gave a little snort and giggle and a short curtsey, as she presented in imagination the wife of the American Minister to an imaginary emperor. There was a loud laugh from the others, and the clever mimic, no longer able to keep up, sank upon the sofa in a paroxysm of mirth.

Mr. and Mrs. Martin had gone down into Maryland a week or so after their arrival, to visit some distant relatives, but they returned a few days before the wedding, and were again domiciled at the house of Madam Benedict, who, much to Zach.'s delight, had once more insisted with much determination, that they should become her guests.

It was the morning of the wedding, and Mr. and Mrs. Martin were alone in the grand parlor, Mrs. M. reclining in a very idle manner on a magnificent sofa, and the old gentlemen gazing about him with astonishment.

"Thunder! what a place it is!" he exclaimed to himself, "a quarter section o' land stocked wouldn't pay for it. Look at the old woman! Acts as if she had been born and cradled in luxury."

Mr. Martin seated himself in a chair and occupied himself in observing his wife.

Mrs. M. touched a bell and a servant appeared.

"A glass of water, Alphonso," she said, sinking back languidly into her place.

"See her!" cried the old gentleman, slapping his legs with delight. "It's better than a show."

"My name be John, ma'am," said the servant, pulling a lock of his hair, and tarrying as if he wanted her to fully understand this important fact before he departed.

"Alphonso is your name," responded Mrs. Martin, severely, "and England is your nation."

"Hingland be my nation, ma'am, but my name be John," he replied.

"Silence!" exclaimed Mrs. Martin.

"Yes'm."

"Go!"

"Yes'm;" and Alphonso, or John, turned hurriedly and left the room.

Mr. Martin was intensely pleased at this. He brought his chair near to where his wife was reclining, and looked at her curiously.

"It's the *best* thing," he exclaimed. Then, bowing very humbly, he said deferentially, "Is your ladyship indisposed?"

Mrs. Martin looked at him severely, but did not answer.

"Be you going to keep at that temperature all the morning, old woman?" he remarked.

"Yes, I be. What then?" said Mrs. Martin.

"Nothing," he responded, "only them high-toned fellers that are coming might git skeered. I should, if I didn't know you, for you look like a regular Lucretia Borgia, and as if you would cut a feller's throat if he winked."

The old lady regarded him with a comical expression, while he looked at her in a broad grin. Then they both rose and began bowing to each other, and finally broke out laughing in great glee.

"Don't I do it pretty well, old man?" said Mrs. Martin.

"You get ahead of anything I ever see," he responded.

"Zach. says," she continued, "I startled everybody that called yesterday, I was so haughty and proud. You see I know a thing or two if I was brought up in a sheep paster. I keep still, and only say 'ye—as' and 'n-o-o,' and they think I could talk as glib as a parrot if I was a mind."

"You look it, old woman; indeed you do," responded her husband.

As they were talking, Zach. entered with a friend, whom he presented to both his father and mother.

"I am glad to meet the parents of my friend," said the gentleman. "How do you like the city, sir?"

"Well, tolerably," replied Mr. Martin. "You see, I ain't used to doing nothing, and it goes a little hard with me, but I s'pose I'd come to like it after awhile."

"Ah! no doubt," responded the other; "as many have done before you. And you, madam," he continued, turning to Mrs. M., "are you favorably impressed?"

"Well, ye — es," replied Mrs. Martin, hesitatingly.

"Oh, I see," said the friend, "You can not speak flatteringly, so you maintain a neutrality?"

"N-o-o!" responded Mrs. M., as if in doubt.

"You will not commit yourself, that's plain," he said. "But you must admire the Capitol?"

"I rather think," replied the old lady, resolving to venture a little, "that it ought to be consolidated."

"What!" he exclaimed, "consol— Ah! I see; pretty good. You refer to the city. Well, it is a little scattered; but it is by no means the city of magnificent distances it was a few years ago."

"There," whispered Mr. Martin to his wife,

pulling her dress. "You got out of that, old woman, but don't try it agin, or you'll ruin it."

An hour afterward Mr. Martin was engaged in a whispered consultation with Peggy in the hall up stairs. "I tell you it won't do," said he. "You just go right along and don't tell him a thing."

"But Mother Martin says he would feel so much better if he knew," pleaded Peggy.

"Mother Martin be hanged!" replied the old gentleman. "I want her to let this business alone· It's too good a joke to spile, and it shan't be spiled."

Whatever the argument was about, Mr. Martin conquered. A short time after that, in the presence of a very few friends, Zachariah Martin and Peggy Clover were made husband and wife.

Peggy looked very beautiful indeed, though she was dressed most inexpensively and wore no ornaments, save a bunch of flowers in her dark hair and at her breast. After the couple had received the congratulations of those present, Peggy disappeared, while Zach. engaged in conversation about their future movements. While he was busy explaining their designs, Peggy, dressed with great richness, appeared at the door. Zach.'s back was toward her, and Judge Spalding stepped up to him and touched him on the arm, interrupting the conversation.

"I beg your pardon, Martin," said the Judge, "but I wish to present to you a friend of mine who has long desired your acquaintance, and one that I trust you will know better in the future."

Peggy had turned her back and bowed her head as Judge Spalding began to speak, but she once more held her face toward them as he said, "Mr. Martin, Miss Margaret Cristopher!" .

For a moment Zach. was stupefied. He looked at the face before him, and then he looked about for Peggy. Then old Mr. Martin, unable to contain himself, began to roar and clap his hands; then Miss Cristopher began half to laugh and half to cry; then they all commenced laughing together, and finally Zach. comprehended the situation.

"Is this possible!" he exclaimed. "Oh, how could I have been so blind! It *was* you, then, and my eyes did not deceive me! Tell me of it — explain it — what does it all mean?"

"Aha, old woman!" cried Mr. Martin. "Peggy is as big a lady as the best of them, after all!"

"I allers thought and prophesied it," returned Mrs. Martin.

Briefly then Peggy recounted her history for the past few years; how she had excited attention with her rough drawing in Philadelphia; how her kind benefactress had first taken an interest in her and accompanied her abroad; how she had in the few years of her pupilage displayed what was thought a wonderful genius for portrait painting, and how she had at last been commissioned by the government and thus made famous.

"I have been on the point of revealing myself to you a dozen times since I have been in Washington," she continued, "but I always hesitated. That you at last married poor little Peggy and none other is a great consolation. But we've had a hard time to keep it, haven't we, Father Martin?" said she, appealing to the old gentleman.

"Like to a busted me," responded Mr. Martin.

"Bless you, Peggy. How little I deserve all this," said Zach.

"You do not deserve it, Martin, that's a fact," said the Judge; "but I can't help it. I have another little duty to perform. I am requested by Madam Benedict to say that she must resign this establishment. It is not hers, but yours, a gift from your wife on your wedding day. She has tried to do the honors so far, but she now gives way and becomes the guest instead of the hostess."

Zach. took out his handkerchief and wiped the perspiration from his face.

"If I ever find words to tell you," said he, taking Peggy by the hand, "how much I "—but his emotion got the better of him, and he turned away to the window.

That evening the beautiful mansion was brilliantly illuminated, and a great company was gathering. The first of our old acquaintances to arrive were Commodore Grimshaw and Mrs. Sampson. They were amazed, of course, and Grimshaw took occasion to tell Zach. that he hoped he would be sent out in command of the iron-clad Podunkinowski to convey him to his new station. Then the gallant Commodore passed on to make room for others, but took up his station so as to observe the arrivals.

"This is the awkward girl that Martin has married," said he to Mrs. Sampson. "There's a nor'wester blowin' to-night."

"I'm struck dumb," responded Mrs. Sampson.

"Mr. and Mrs. and Miss Marmaluke," shouted the servant. Zach. started. He had not expected them, but he hardly had time to think before they came in and were presented.

"I congratulate you, Martin," said Mr. Marmaluke.

"Oh, all of us!" exclaimed Mrs. Marmaluke. "We are delighted."

"Thank you," responded Zach.

Then they were presented in turn to Peggy.

As they looked, both Belle and her mother gave a start and seemed absolutely to grow faint.

"That's a shot from the bow gun," growled Grimshaw, who was watching them.

The crowd passed on, and in the course of things, old Mr. and Mrs. Martin came in for many introductions. As these began to grow frequent Mr. Martin whispered, "Keep up your resolution, old woman, and don't speak. This is getting thick."

"Look out for yourself, Joseph," replied she, "and let me alone."

"Good evening, ladies!" said the old Commodore, as Belle and her mother approached him. "You look happy to-night. That's right. I like to see people merry over the success of their friends. How do you like the looks of Mrs. Martin?"

"We have met her before," returned Belle, coldly. "She was formerly Miss Cristopher."

"But *we* didn't know it before. Did you, Miss Marmaluke?" said Grimshaw.

"Well, we know it now, I suppose," she answered.

"Yes, we all know it now, and are so much pleased over it!" said he, provokingly.

Belle turned away and consulted with her mother.

"Mr. G. Henry Audley, Mrs. Barker, Mrs. Gammill!" cried the servant at the door.

"There goes a whole broadside," said the Commodore to his companion. "It'll sweep their decks clean. They'll all strike their flags and surrender in a minute."

Audley was utterly prostrated when he was presented to Mrs. Martin, late Miss Cristopher. He staggered, and rubbed his eyes in amazement. As for Mrs. Barker, she became very red in the face, and the smile which she had prepared herself to reveal, never troubled her at all.

"What is there vulgar about his parents?" said Mrs. Marmaluke to Belle a few minutes later, as if determined to make herself as miserable as possible. "He seems to be a very sensible old gentleman, and as for Martin's mother, she's a born aristocrat."

Just here Audley was presented to the old lady, and the two went bowing about with great gusto.

"What a perlite young creetur it is," whispered the old lady to her husband.

"Well, I *am* suffocated," remarked Mrs. Barker to Belle when she got to the latter's side. "The ignorant girl is a queen, and the queen of Washington society. What can it mean? How did it come about?"

"My hopes are blasted," remarked Audley, approaching, with a look of great dejection. "I shall retire from the world."

"Courage," said Mrs. Barker. "They say she has a sister. When neckties fail in one quarter they may win in another." But the young man refused to be comforted, and grew very limp and melancholy.

"Colonel Ebenezer Barncastle, A. B., F. R. S.," shouted the servant. There was a stir, for this

was not a familiar name in such gatherings. Zach.
and Peggy, however, smiled good humoredly.

Barncastle came in with the same airy swing
as ever, and seemed quite at home in the brilliant
assemblage.

"Forgive me, my friend," said he, taking the
hand of Zach. "I am without a card, but friendship can overlook conventionalities. Depart from
the land you have honored by your life, and will
drape in mourning at your death, with the benediction of Barncastle."

"I am glad to welcome you," said Zach., "and
to thank you for the services you rendered my
wife and myself."

" In her friendlessness," said Barncastle, loftily,
"temporary but pitiful, I may say, I protected her.
I made her cause and your cause my own, and
brought her through the — what I may call the
wilderness, into the promised land. Eh, right?"

"Mr. Barncastle," said Zach., crossing over to
where his father and mother stood, "let me present you to my parents."

"What!" exclaimed Barncastle, falling back, and gazing with admiration upon them. "Do I indeed behold the proud and happy parents of a rising statesman? Madam, your hand; let me grasp with an emotion I can not disguise the honored palm of a proud and happy mother."

"What a splendid man!" said Mrs. Martin, "He's the only one among 'em who talks like a book."

"And you, honest granger!" continued Barncastle, holding the hand of Zach.'s father; "venerable agriculturist, *your* hand. You hold in your grasp, sir, the destinies of this republic!"

Mr. Martin looked down into his hand as if to see whether such a mighty settlement had been made there since he last observed it.

"You must fight the battles of liberty," pursued Barncastle. "Upon the honest yeomanry of the land the nation casts its despairing glance. Organize, sir; organize everwhere. Organize in every school district; in every hamlet; in every quarter of the land, and let your motto be: 'Our country! May she ever be right; but right or wrong, our country.'"

Barncastle subsided, and Mr. Martin turned to his wife with a quizzical smile. " Talks exactly like Snyder did when he ran for Sheriff," said he.

There was a very fine banquet later in the evening, and as it neared the close a member of the House rose and proposed the health of Zach. He reviewed his political career, indulged in a good deal of fulsome praise, and concluded by prophesying a brilliant future for the Martin's Corners statesman. Zach. rose to respond with much applause. There was a happy, contented look upon his face, but no signs of undue elation. He spoke very calmly, very modestly, very sensibly; in fact, more sensibly, perhaps, than ever before in his life. The blows he had received had been severe indeed, but they had broken the shell of vanity and self-adulation that had surrounded him, and exposed the true metal in the man at last. He thanked the speaker for his kind words and those present for their

kind wishes, and then continued: " The President has been kind enough to appoint me to
a position of honor and responsibility abroad, and
you have been kind enough to congratulate me
thereon. My friends, the little misfortunes which
I have undergone may have made me unneces-
sarily timid or foolishly apprehensive. I know not;
but just now I feel indisposed to re-enter public
life. To tell the truth, I have become satisfied
that I am not a statesman (he never was so near
it as at that moment), and I assure you that it
does not pain me any longer to know that in this
opinion the people seem to concur. The happiness and satisfaction which I looked for in public
life are not there, my friends, at least for me. I
doubt much if they are there for any. To even
the highest, the purest, the best, there are draughts
of bitterness which must make the partakers long
for that cup of peace which is reserved alone for
independence. I could moralize on this theme,
but I will not. The public is as it is, and it will
remain so. If I can in an humble capacity do

19   C2

anything to soften criticism, to temper denunciation, and to encourage charity toward public servants, who are always fallible, to be sure, but not
always vile, I shall feel that I have found a sphere
in life better suited to my abilities than the one I
am now leaving. For some of these reasons I
shall not accept the mission which has been tendered me, but for which I am nevertheless most
grateful."

Here the audience gave a start of genuine surprise.

."No," continued Zach. "Away back in the
West is a humble, rural home, where I was happy
as a boy and where I hope to be happy as a man.
Not that I wish or expect to become a recluse, or
shut myself up in cynical solitude. But there are
other duties, other aims in life besides those which
direct us here. And back there where she, who
has to-night united her fortunes with mine, and
your speaker were reared, among those who have
known us so long and well, we shall take up our
home. And so, my friends, I lay down my political

ambition, and, as I do so, part with an anxiety which I have borne like Christian's burden for years. I am no longer a target for sportsmen. I am a sportsman myself, but humane and considerate, I hope, from a knowledge of the pain which poisoned arrows can inflict. Though I talk gravely, I need scarcely say to you that my heart is very light. I have tried all things. I hold fast to that which is good. If I have never done wisely before, I feel the conviction that I do wisely now."

Zach. took Peggy by the hand as he said this, and after thanking his friends again, and extending an invitation to them to visit him in his home, took his seat.

Thus did Zachariah Martin begin and end his public career. The next day, in the midst of preparations for leaving, a carriage drove up to the door, and there alighted Mrs. Marmaluke, Belle, and Judge Spalding, The two ladies entered the parlor with blanched faces, and on Zach.'s appearance Mrs. Marmaluke burst into tears and besought Zach. to save her daughter. Zach. was amazed, and presently Judge Spalding explained. An indictment had been found against Hartwell and Belle for bribery, the penalty for offering a bribe being the same as for receiving one. Belle was therefore in danger of a disgraceful arrest if not an actual term in the penitentiary. Hartwell had incontinently fled. Judge Spalding informed Zach. that with his consent he would take it upon himself to see that no arrest was made, and that the case could be "nolle prossed" when it came up. The assurance was at once given by Zach. that, so far as he was concerned, no steps should be taken toward any prosecution, and so the matter ended. As Belle took his hand and thanked him, or tried to thank him, the tears came into her eyes, albeit unused to such companions, and her voice faltered and gave way, and then her old lover bowed very low to her, and so she passed from his presence for probably the last time.

A word or two and we end our story. Zach. and Peggy have retired to the old farm, and there,

surrounded with many of the luxuries of the life
they have left, they pass their Summers. They
have for a companion one other beside old Mr.
and Mrs. Martin, and that is Madam Benedict.
Regarding Peggy as a daughter, Mrs. Benedict
will not consent to be separated from her, and so
insists that Peggy and Zach., and not unfrequently
Mr. and Mrs. Martin, shall spend their Winters
with her in Philadelphia, while she passes the
Summer with them on the farm. Old Mr. Martin
thinks there is rather too much play and too little
work about all this, but the old lady enjoys the
arrangement hugely, and except on momentous
occasions she always has her way. Peggy is
engaged on a very pretentious landscape scene
now, and has high hopes of succeeding even better
in this line than in that of portrait painting. She
and Zach. both declare that they have found the
true level at last, and that they are thrice as happy
as if they had never been tried in the fire. Spiker
is still engaged in politics, and is talking very loud
about this year's campaign. He has fallen out

with the present member, and actually addressed a note to Zach. soliciting him to become a candidate, an invitation which the latter very firmly, but good-naturedly, declined.

Audley is married — married to an estimable young lady, too, who has strong hopes of making something of him yet. "It's the strangest thing how he came to marry her," he says, and everybody agrees with him without hesitation.

Hartwell committed a forgery a short time ago, and left the country, it is hoped never to return.

Belle is still in society, and may be seen at almost every fashionable reception in Washington, a little faded and ancient, but still with her share of admirers. The prospect of an eligible match for her is growing decidedly dim, but Mrs. Marmaluke still has hope.

It was only a short time ago that Zach. received the following letter, which he read with much amusement:

NEW YORK CITY, —— 18—.

MUCH HONORED AND DEAR SIR: I drop you a line to inform you that I too, taking your bright example for my guide, have retired from politics. It is fascinating but dangerous. I am now engaged in the great Zoological and Moral Museum, at the street and number hereto appended. I in a great measure organized the enterprise, and it is now my duty to describe to passing pedestrians the wonders of our collection, and invite them into the most gigantic and gorgeous exhibition now before the public. (Admission 25 cents; children under 10 years half price.) I assure you, Mr. Martin, that here is a field for talent of which I little dreamed when floundering amid the sloughs of Congressional life. The innocent gaities of the monkey tribe, the deep repose of the anaconda, and the native dignity of the ourang-outang, form a peaceful and happy spectacle most refreshing to a worn-out statesman. If you visit New York drop in and see them. A child can handle the entire collection with the utmost safety. Remember me to your distinguished consort, and believe me gratefully, and with high consideration, your friend,

EBENEZER BARNCASTLE.
Professor of Zoology.

Mr. and Mrs. Zachariah Martin will certainly visit Barncastle when they go to New York.

The family of little Bobbin are living at Martin's Corners, and, thanks to Zach. and Peggy, in very comfortable circumstances. Bobbin's death was regretted by all who knew him, and there was sincere grief when his remains were laid away in the little churchyard.

By Peggy's direction a beautiful monument has been erected to his memory, and on it appears the following simple inscription:

TIMOTHY BOBBIN,

AGED 34.

" He found the cup of life too bitter,
And turned away his head."

THE WIFE WINS.

By R. G. Burdette, of the "Burlington Hawkeye."

When they reached the depot, Mr. Mann and his wife gazed in unspeakable disappointment at the receding train, which was just pulling away from the bridge-switch at the rate of a thousand miles a minute. The first impulse was to run after it, but as the train was out of sight and whistling for Sagetown before they could act upon the impulse, they remained in the carriage, and disconsolately turned their horses' heads homeward.

"It all comes of having to wait for a woman to get ready," Mr. Mann broke the silence very grimly.

"I was ready before you were," replied his wife.

"Great heavens!" cried Mr. Mann, with keen impatience, jerking the horses' jaws out of place; "just listen to that. I sat in the buggy ten minutes, yelling at you to come along, until the whole neighborhood heard me."

"Yes," acquiesced Mrs. Mann, with the provoking placidity that none can assume but a woman, "and every time I started down stairs you sent me back for something you had forgotten."

Mr. Mann groaned. "This is too much to bear," he said, "when everybody knows that if I were going to Europe I would rush into the house, put on a clean shirt, grab up my grip-sack and fly, while you would want at least six months for preliminary preparations, and then dawdle around the whole day of starting until every train had left town."

Well, the upshot of the matter was, that the Manns put off their visit to Aurora until the next week, and it was agreed that each one should get himself or herself ready and go down to the train and go; and the one who failed to get ready should be left. The day of the match came around in due time. The train was going at 10.30, and Mann, after attending to his business, went home at 9.45.

"Now, then," he shouted, "only three-quarters of an hour's time. Fly around; a fair field and no favors, you know."

And away they flew. Mr. Mann bulged into this room and flew through that one, and dived into one closet after another with inconceivable rapidity, chuckling under his breath all the time to think how cheap Mrs. Mann would feel when he started off alone. He stopped on his way up stairs to pull off his heavy boots to save time. For the same reason he pulled off his coat, and he ran through the dining room and hung it on a corner of the silver closet. Then he jerked off his vest as he rushed through the hall, and tossed it on a hook in the hat rack, and by the time he had reached his own room he was ready to plunge into his clean clothes. He pulled out the bureau drawer and began to paw at the things like a Scotch terrier after a rat.

"Eleanor," he shrieked, "where are my shirts?"

"In your bureau drawer," calmly replied Mrs. Mann, who was standing before a glass, quietly and deliberately coaxing a refractory crimp into place.

"Well, by thunder, they ain't," shouted Mr. Mann, a little annoyed. "I've emptied everything out of the drawer, and there isn't a thing in it I ever saw before."

Mrs. Mann stepped back a few paces, held her head on one side, and after satisfying herself that the crimp would do, and would stay where she had put it, replied:

"These things scattered around on the floor are all mine. Probably you haven't be·n looking in your own drawer."

"I don't see," testily observed Mr. Mann, "why you couldn't have put my things out for me, when you had nothing else to do all the morning."

"Because," said Mrs. Mann, settling herself into an additional article of raiment with awful deliberation, "nobody put mine out for me. A fair field and no favors, my dear."

Mr. Mann plunged into his shirt like a bull at a red flag.

"Foul!" he shouted in malicious triumph. · "No buttons on the neck!"

"Because," said Mrs. Mann, sweetly, after a deliberate stare at the fidgeting, impatient man, during which she buttoned her dress and put eleven pins where they would do the most good, "because you have got the shirt on wrong side out."

When Mr. Mann slid out of the shirt he began to sweat. He dropped the shirt three times before he got it on, and while it was over his head he heard the clock strike ten. When his head came through he saw Mrs. Mann coaxing the ends and bows of her necktie.

"Where's my shirt studs?" he cried.

Mrs. Mann went out into another room, and presently came back with her gloves and her hat, and saw Mr. Mann emptying all the boxes he could find in and about the bureau. Then she said:

"In the shirt you just pulled off."

Mrs. Mann put on her gloves while Mr. Mann hunted up and down the room for his cuff buttons.

"Eleanor," he snarled at last, "I believe you must know where those cuff buttons are."

"I haven't seen them," said the lady, settling her hat, "didn't you lay them down on the window sill in the sitting room last night?"

Mr. Mann remembered, and went down stairs on the run. He stepped on one of his boots, and was immediately landed in the hall at the foot of the stairs with neatness and dispatch, attended in the transmission with more bumps than he could count with Weob's adder, and landing with a bang like the Hell Gate explosion.

"Are you nearly ready, Algernon?" asked the wife of his family, sweetly, leaning over the banisters.

· The unhappy man groaned. "Can you throw me down the other boot?" he asked.

Mrs. Mann pityingly kicked it down to him.

"My valise?" he inquired, as he tugged at the boot.

"Up in your dressing room," she answered.

"Packed?"

"I do not know; unless you packed it yourself, probably not," she replied, with her hand on the door knob; "I had barely time to pack my own."

She was passing out of the gate, when the door opened, and he shouted:

"Where in the name of goodness did you put my vest! It has all of my money in it."

"You threw it on the hat rack," she called; "good-bye, dear."

Before she reached the corner of the street she was hailed again:

"Eleanor! Eleanor! Eleanor Mann! Did you wear off my coat?"

She paused and turned, after signaling the street car to stop, and cried:

"You threw it on the silver closet."

And the street car engulphed her graceful form, and she was seen no more. But the neighbors say that they heard Mr. Mann charging up and down the house, rushing out of the front door every now and then, shrieking up the deserted street after the unconscious Mrs. Mann, to know where his hat was, and where she put the valise key, and if he had any clean socks and undershirts, and that there wasn't a linen collar in the house. And when he went away at last, he left the kitchen door, the side door, and the front door, all the downstairs windows and the front gate wide open; and the loungers around the depot were somewhat amused, just as the train was pulling out of sight down in the yards to see a flushed, perspiring man, with his hat on sideways, his vest buttoned two buttons too high, his cuffs unbuttoned and necktie flying, and his gripsack flapping open and shut like a demented shutter on a March night, and a door key in his hand, dash wildly across the platform and halt in the middle of the track, glaring in dejected, impotent, wrathful mortification at the departing train, and shaking his fist at a pretty woman who was throwing kisses at him from the rear platform of the last car.

www.ingramcontent.com/pod-product-compliance
Lightning Source LLC
Chambersburg PA
CBHW032259280326
41932CB00009B/632